ON THE COMPOSITION OF
PARADISE LOST

ON THE COMPOSITION OF

PARADISE LOST

A STUDY OF THE ORDERING
AND INSERTION OF
MATERIAL

BY

ALLAN H. GILBERT

"la tela novella ch'ora ordisco"
PETRARCH, Sonnet XXXII

1972

OCTAGON BOOKS
New York

Reprinted 1966

by special arrangement with The University of North Carolina Press

Second Octagon Printing 1972

OCTAGON BOOKS

A DIVISION OF FARRAR, STRAUS & GIROUX, INC.

19 Union Square West

New York, N. Y. 10003

LIBRARY OF CONGRESS CATALOG CARD NUMBER: 66-18048

ISBN 0-374-93059-7

Printed in U.S.A. by

NOBLE OFFSET PRINTERS, INC.

NEW YORK 3, N. Y.

THIS STUDY IS DEDICATED
TO THE MEMORY OF MY FATHER
EDDY C. GILBERT
WHO UNWITTINGLY GAVE ME OPPORTUNITY
FOR ITS COMPOSITION

PREFACE

To some readers of the following study it doubtless will appear that the foundation is not enough to carry the superstructure. The evidence is found chiefly in inconsistencies in *Paradise Lost;* some of them are slight inconsistencies; slight certainly, if the word means that they do not materially injure the poem. Yet they exist, and they are not too slight to support the conclusions drawn from them. Short of statements by an author or his friends or of a series of his manuscripts, there can be little evidence on composition save what is internal. Though some of my inferences from this evidence may be mistaken, I hope they will not be condemned until the poem as a whole and the particular passages in question have been critically re-read. None of my observations is intended to be dogmatic. Indeed I expect—at least wish—that others will modify them, if only they do so in moving toward better understanding of *Paradise Lost* and of poetry generally. If in my zeal I have sometimes spoken overpositively, I trust that the tolerant reader will allow that I do not really imagine I acted as Milton's secretary. If I have sometimes found inconsistencies where there are none, so much the better for Milton's workmanship. My attempt has been "to save appearances," to find a way of explaining what stands in the poem. Some readers may feel that my efforts are as much worth laughter as were those of the non-Copernican astronomers; I shall be glad to yield to anyone who has the simple and adequate solution. Doubtless, too, I have overlooked evidence, perhaps sufficient to change some of my conclusions, all of which are absolute only in their recognition that Milton's great achievement shows marks of the labor with which it was constructed.

My study rests on and—if acceptable—returns to a view of Milton's character. There is an old tradition of an icily perfect Milton in his singing robes

> Above the smoke and stir of this dim spot
> Which men call earth.

This as an exclusive interpretation has received some heavy blows in the last thirty-five or forty years, but like many inheritances from eighteenth- and nineteenth-century criticism, is still powerful. Milton was "classical" if the word means that he took great pains to plan his work as a totality before he began to write. But did he allow his inventive powers to rest when he began to compose verses? It seems to me that he was always ready for Urania to return with something fresh, that he was willing to make continual changes of every sort, that he felt no condescension in cutting and patching. The page from *Comus* reproduced in Figure 5 does not look like the work of a man whose Minerva sprang full-grown from his brain, even though that page apparently was written as a fair copy. To me a Milton who was willing to shift and change is a better artist than one who wrote once and for all with superhuman certainty; at least he would be a pleasanter one to meet.

> Thy soul was like a Star, and dwelt apart . . .
> So didst thou travel on life's common way . . .
> The lowliest duties . . .

*

I wish to express my thanks to the Research Council of Duke University and to Professor Marcia L. Anderson, Dr. Josephine W. Bennett, Dr. Freda Townsend, Mr. Oswald E. Davies, Mr. Ralph Nash, Professor George Coffin Taylor, Dr. A. C. Howell, and Miss Mary Olive Thomas.

CONTENTS

INTRODUCTION

What do poets do when they compose? It is known that they revise, but most of the study of their revision has been given to verbal details. Even more important is change of plan, causing transfer or insertion of blocks of material. Yet this has been less observed than smaller variations, partly because the rough manuscripts showing it are less likely to be kept than later ones with merely verbal alterations. Though such major changes are usually hidden, Mrs. Bennett, in *The Evolution of the Faerie Queene*, has shown that Spenser in his later books used material written earlier than some of that in the first three. After her study it is no longer possible for a critic to assume that any author of a long and labored poem such as *Paradise Lost* composed in the present sequence of the work. The burden of proof for seriatim composition rests upon him.

Though, as Conington says of studies of the order of composition of the books of the *Aeneid*, examination of the conformity of part with part concerns "the critical scholar rather than the general reader," the process is not that of a Zoilus, taking pleasure in collecting the defects of Homer. It is the observing of the poet as he works, with the pleasure of seeing how he substituted the better for the good. Learning all he can about the poem from without, examining any manuscripts the author has left, but above all, interrogating the finished work itself, the critic endeavors to gain from it the secrets of its building. He finds indications of the author's earliest intention in a part that has survived many revisings. In another and newer section, that purpose has become clearer though perhaps more complex. In the last additions it has reached its final form. Older parts have been re-

3

vised enough to bring them at least superficially into harmony with it. Subsidiary purposes have been taken up, modified, perhaps discarded, still leaving traces, perhaps very faint, of their existence. Sections that once came near the beginning of the poem have been shifted to the middle or the end and late passages have now become initial. Some of these processes are so complete that only a guess can be made, others have left indications so slight as hardly to be found, a few are virtually certain. If he has assurance of a few, the critic can guess with probability at others, at least can come to realize the general nature of the process. It is as though he frequently was with the poet in his workshop, watching the processes of construction and of finishing and polishing. Much of the artist's work is done in the critic's absence, but what the watcher sees gives him an intimacy with the poem invaluable in forming judgments. He shares with the author secrets of composition such as the simple reader, looking only at the finished product, cannot attain. He knows what parts are essential to the effect as the artist last imagined it and what ones express earlier and now vanished phases.

Yet critics have generally not taken saltatory composition into account. It has been conventional to say that the first book of *Paradise Lost* is the work of John Milton fresh at his task and Book XII his product when he was worn down by much writing. But before believing this we must know that he composed the poem in its present sequence. Style is not to be called early or late merely because it occurs near the beginning or the end of the epic.

Moreover, continuing and repeated change, in passages both long and short, executed over a number of years and involving addition, excision, and shifting of material—all by a blind man dependent on the eyes and brain of an amanuensis—could not but leave on the finished work marks that can be called defects.[1] Though it is proper for interpreters to fix their attention chiefly on the merits of *Paradise Lost*, they can hardly give a just estimate if they so insist on flawless workmanship as to overlook human inconsistencies and slips of memory inevitable in the course of years of labor. An example may be found in the story of Abdiel. As will be later explained, there is reason to think that this angel was not in Milton's early plan but was added as

1. See Sec. 51, below.

the poet's views enlarged.[2] As the narrative now stands, Abdiel, meeting Satan in single combat, gains a clear advantage, so that the rebel leader is "foiled." In spite of this, it is later said that Satan, until his unhappy contest with Michael, had "met in Armes No equal" (VI. 247-48). Puzzled by the contradiction, Newton wrote a note that has been taken over by some of his successors:

The poet seems almost to have forgotten how Satan was foil'd by Abdiel in the beginning of the action: but I suppose the poet did not consider Abdiel as *equal* to Satan, tho' he gain'd that accidental advantage over him. Satan no doubt would have prov'd an overmatch for Abdiel, only for the general engagement which ensued, and broke off the combat between them.

This explanation is merely the annotator's supposition; Milton gives no basis for making the advantage gained by Abdiel accidental or Satan his overmatch. On the contrary the angel says in soliloquy:

> His puissance, trusting in th' Almightie's aide,
> I mean to try, whose Reason I have tri'd
> Unsound and false; nor is it aught but just,
> That he who in debate of Truth hath won,
> Should win in Arms, in both disputes alike
> Victor.   (VI. 119-24)

When the story of Abdiel is looked on as a late insertion, the matter is clear. Satan as without equal belongs to an early stratum, in which the leaders of the hosts fight in Homeric fashion. Abdiel was added when Milton wished to express in action the superiority of truth, to which the angel as servant of God is devoted. The poet did indeed forget, as Newton guessed, but in a direction opposite to the one the commentator suggests. He did not forget Abdiel when he wrote of Michael, but when he inserted Abdiel he forgot that he should modify Satan's combat with Michael. In such an instance, to rationalize for the sake of consistency is to wreck the poem. It is better that a lapse be recognized as such rather than that irreconcilable passages be forced into agreement.

The flaws pointed out are hardly to be called defects; they indicate the process of achieving greater excellence, are deviations from the

2. See Sec. 37, below.

mathematical that make the work of the hand more attractive than that of the machine, tokens of the humanity that the artist shares with his readers. So the critic, if he estimates his function aright, regards them. When he too, as sometimes he must if he is to judge as man and not as mere technician, becomes also the general reader, these flaws vanish in the poet's entire achievement. To recognize them helps in the characterization of the work by which the critic aids men generally when, from direct aesthetic enjoyment, they turn to the rational approach that the questioning human mind soon or late insists upon.

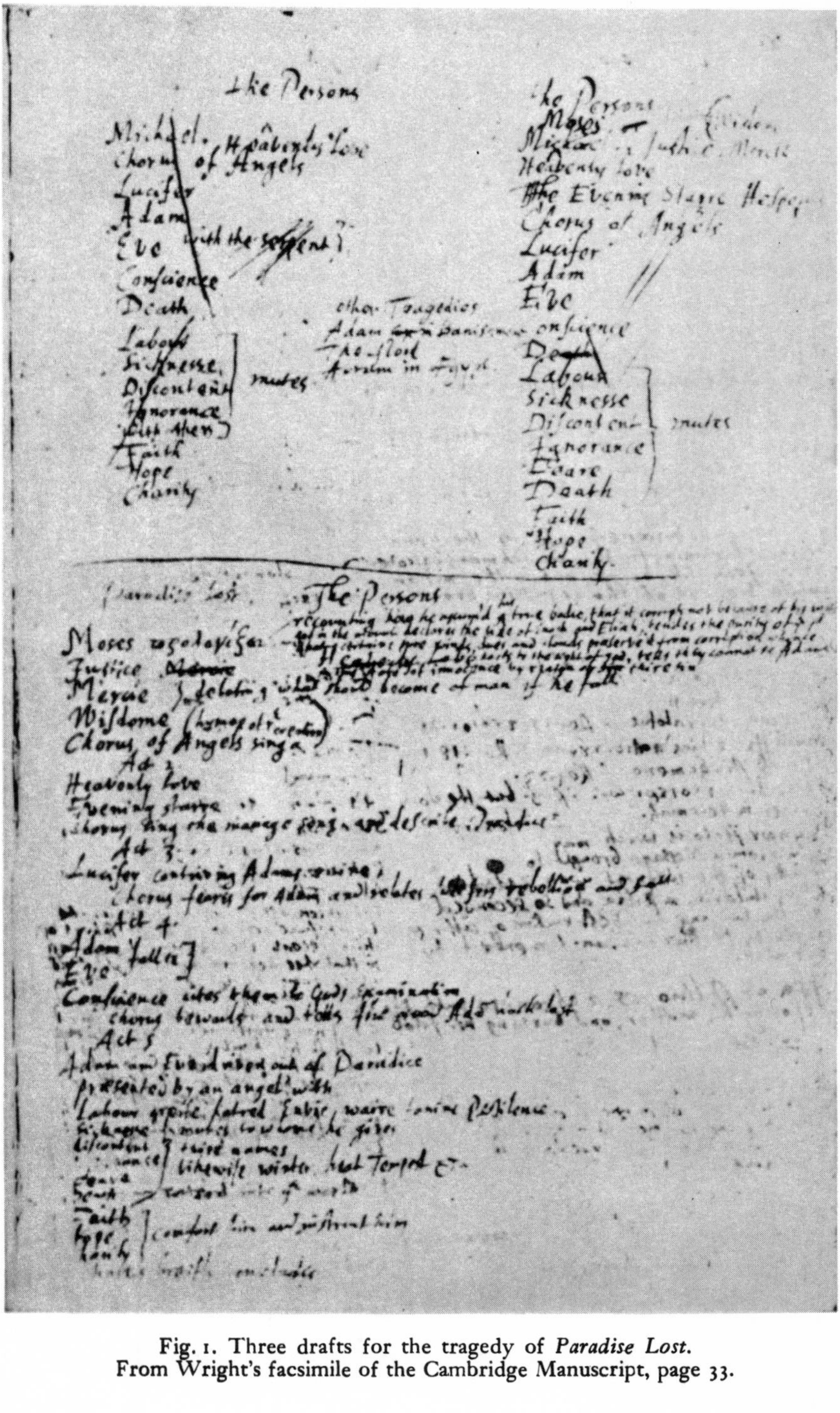

Fig. 1. Three drafts for the tragedy of *Paradise Lost*.
From Wright's facsimile of the Cambridge Manuscript, page 33.

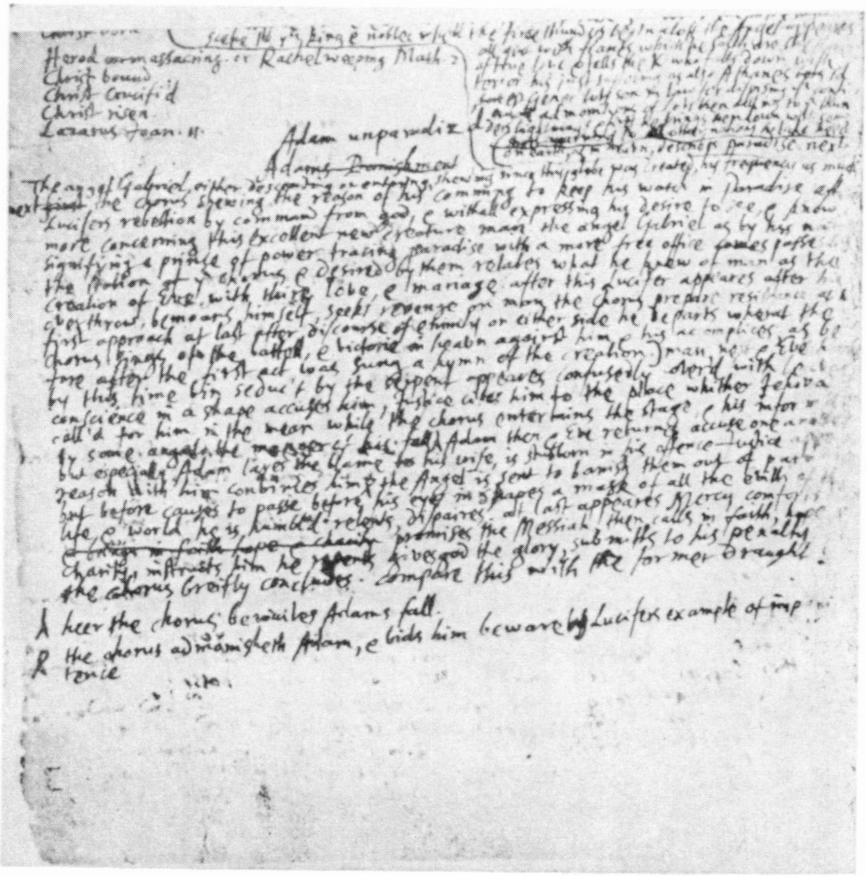

Fig. 2. The draft for the tragedy of *Adam unparadiz'd*.
From Wright's facsimile, page 38.

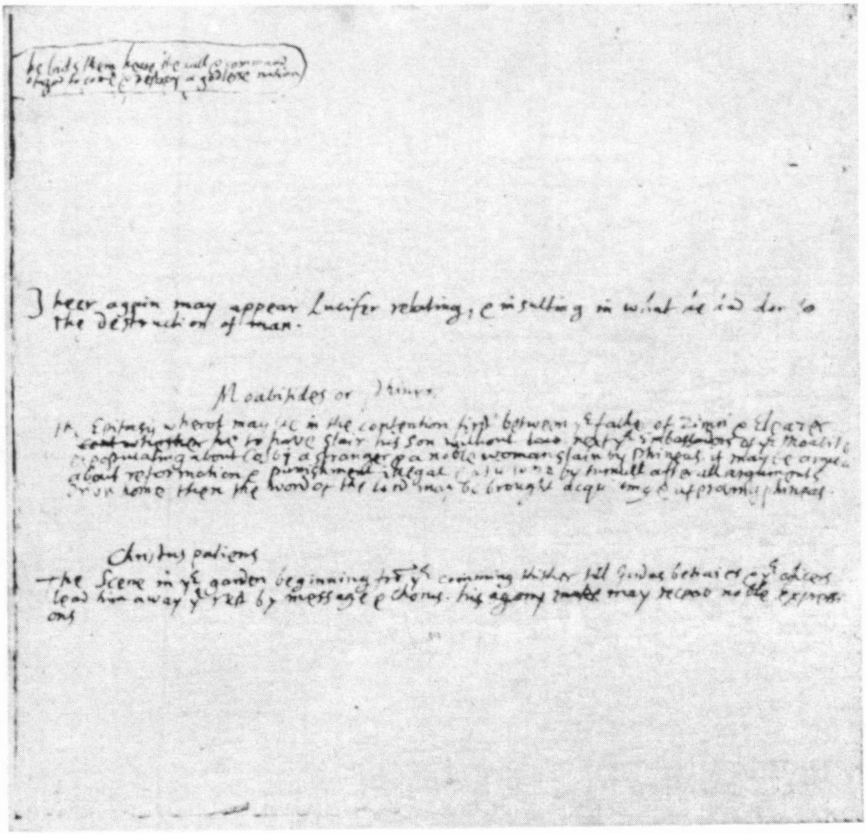

Fig. 3. Milton's additions to the draft for the tragedy of *Adam unparadiz'd*.
From Wright's facsimile, page 39.

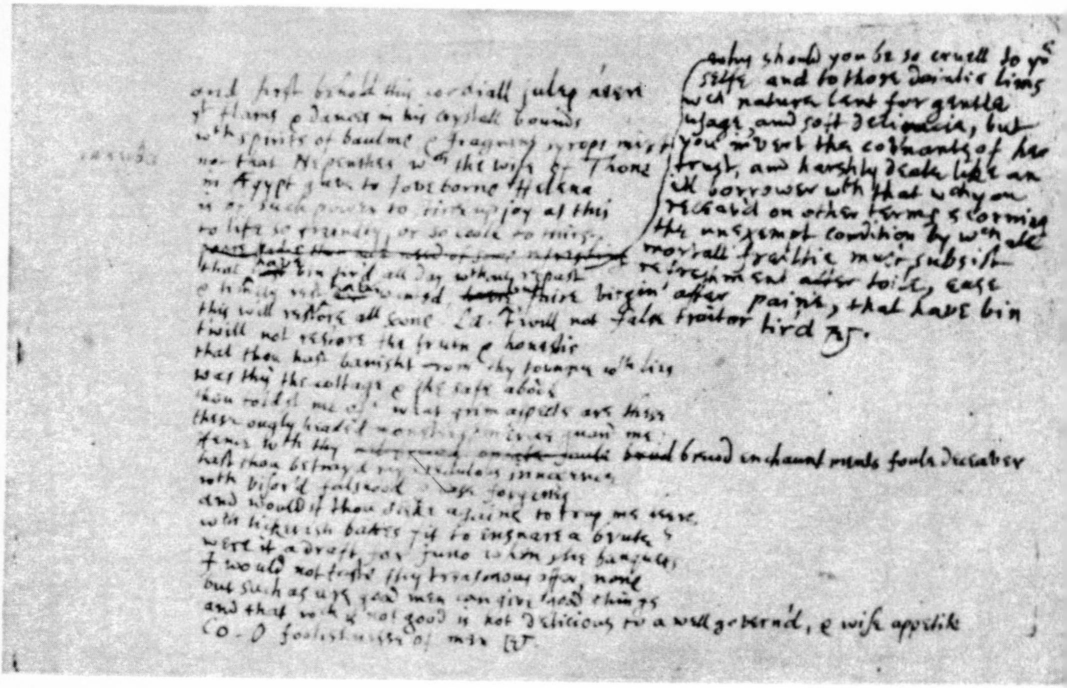

Fig. 4. Milton's revisions of *Comus*, lines 671-705. From Wright's facsimile, page 20. This and Figure 5 show how the young Milton revised details. After he became blind he must in some equivalent way have revised his later work.

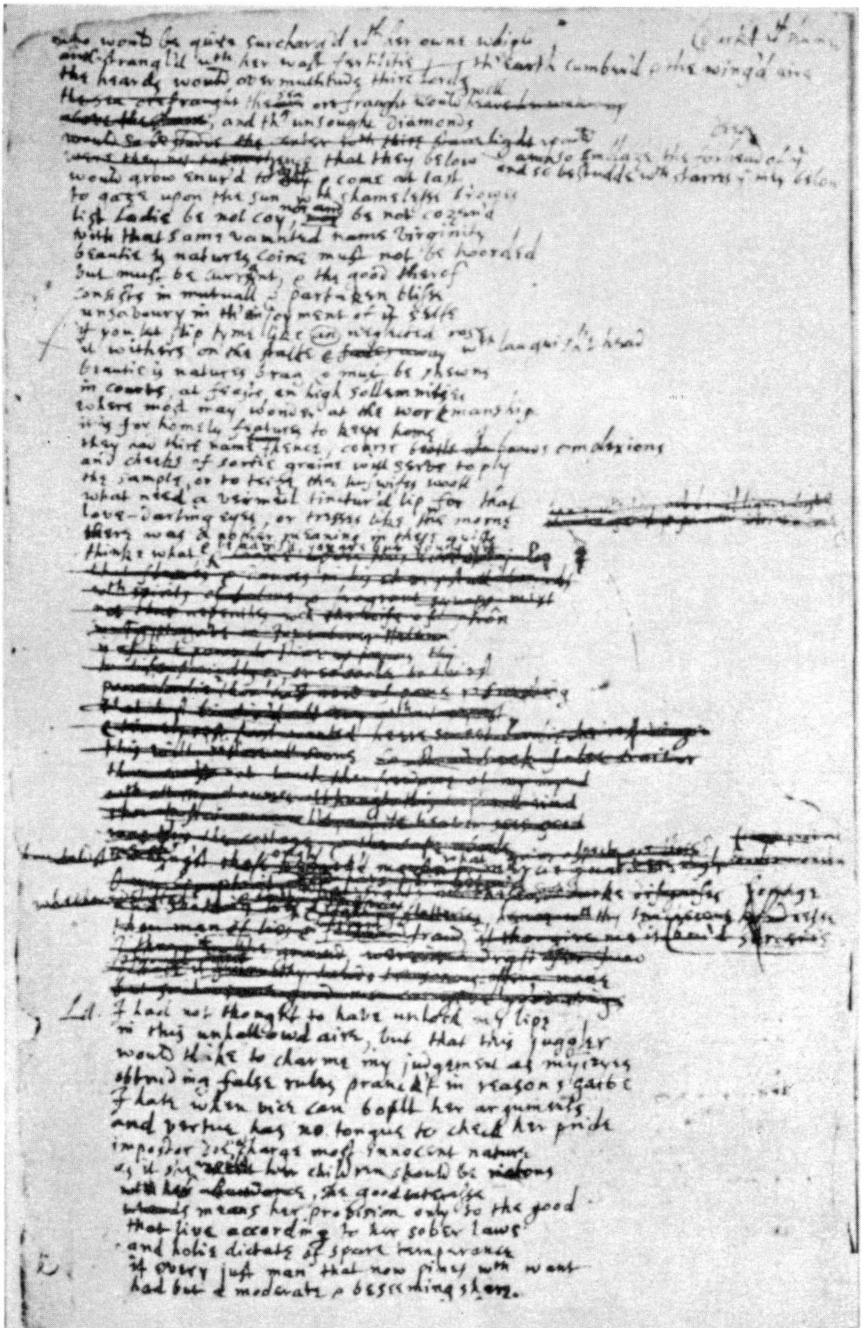

Fig. 5. Milton's revisions of *Comus*, lines 727-768.
From Wright's facsimile, page 22.

CHAPTER ONE

LONG CHOOSING

1. How Milton Composed

A NUMBER of years passed by while Milton—always handi-capped by his blindness—was composing his epic. During this period he was interrupted by other writing, especially the *Treatise of Civil Power in Ecclesiastical Causes*, the *Considerations Touching the Likeliest Means to Remove Hirelings out of the Church*, and the *Readie and Easie Way to Establish a Free Commonwealth*. Moreover Edward Phillips reports his uncle as saying "That his Vein never happily flow'd, but from the *Autumnal Equinoctial* to the *Vernal*, and that whatever he attempted was never to his satisfaction, though he courted his fancy never so much; so that in all the years he was about this Poem, he may be said to have spent but half his time therein."[1]

We know little of his procedure when he was composing freely. Apparently he did not produce long passages in a single burst, but only a few lines at a time. Edward Phillips writes: "I had the perusal of [*Paradise Lost*] from the very beginning; for some years, as I went from time to time, to Visit him, in a Parcel of Ten, Twenty, or Thirty Verses at a Time."[2] Suggesting more rapid work, though perhaps too late to be taken seriously, is Richardson's account: "I have been also told he would Dictate many, perhaps 40 Lines as it were in a Breath, and then reduce them to half the Number."[3] This also indicates the

1. Edward Phillips, *The Life of Mr. John Milton*, in Helen Darbishire, *The Early Lives of Milton* (London, 1932), p. 73.
2. *Ibid.*
3. *Life of Milton*, in Darbishire, *op. cit.*, p. 291. Is it possible that this story is influenced by the following on Vergil: "Cum Georgica scriberet, traditur co-

completion of only twenty lines. Much work on small units, and that greatly interrupted, would take the poet's attention from the larger matters of his plan.

Of that planning the biographers have told nothing. Yet the "oiconomie" required no small amount of thought, since even when after "long choosing" the subject had been decided on, there still remained the problem whether "the rules of *Aristotle* herein are strictly to be kept, or nature to be follow'd, which in them that know art, and use judgment is no transgression, but an inriching of art."[4] The outlines for tragedies in the Cambridge Manuscript lead to the guess that an outline for the epic as well early took written form—liable, however, to change. How much replanning did the scheme of *Paradise Lost* actually undergo as composition proceeded? This can only be inferred from the finished work. Further, to what extent did Milton write his poem in the order of even a shifting outline, and to what extent did he write sections when the spirit moved? Having early decided that Adam should learn something of the future, is it not possible that he wrote the eleventh and twelfth books before he presented Satan in Hell? It is likely that some of Milton's composition was saltatory rather than steady and consecutive.[5]

tidie meditatos mane plurimos versus dictare solitus, ac per totum diem retractando ad paucissimos redigere, non absurde carmen se ursae more parere dicens et lambendo demum effingere."— Suetonius, *De Viris Inlustribus*, XXVb, ed. Reifferscheid (Leipzig, 1860), p. 59.

4. *The Reason of Church-government*, Preface to Book II, Columbia ed., Vol. III, Pt. I, p. 237.

5. Professor McColley writes: "Should the five years of actual composition have fallen largely within the three eras of 1652-53, 1655-58, and 1660-63, we may expect evidence of disjunctive composition within the poem. As all writers know too well, disjoined composition invites inconsistencies which the greatest care does not always locate.

Handicapped by blindness, Milton would have found their detecting unusually difficult. . . .

"Our inquiry is now confronted with a problem untouched by Miltonic scholarship: Did the poet compose the books and sections of *Paradise Lost* in the order in which they appeared in his published version? . . . Evidence . . . suggests that the order of publication was not the order of composition. . . .

"Necessarily conjectural are my conclusions regarding the order in which Milton composed the first three-fifths of the epic. Evidence chiefly internal, but supported by *Adam unparadiz'd* and the abandoned tragedy, suggests strongly that Books I-III, the third quarter of Book IV, and the first two-thirds of Book V

Some parts of *Paradise Lost* may have been composed as independent poems. We do not know what papers may have been in Milton's desk about 1655. If the additions made in 1673 to the poems first printed in 1645 are evidence, there was not much remaining that was suitable to go among his shorter works. In addition to his sonnets, Milton then had translations of the Psalms and youthful poems. There is no trace of any longer poems. Some of the dramas outlined in the Cambridge Manuscript may have been on paper, but we do not know. Dreams of poetry are spread before us in *The Reason of Church-government*, yet there is no evidence, aside from the published poems, that they were other than dreams. It is reported that Spenser composed various works, such as his *Epithalamium Thamesis*, that can be identified in the *Faerie Queene*.[6] But for Milton we know only that he contemplated a poem on King Arthur, not that he wrote any of it. Examination of *Paradise Lost* for such incorporated parts is not rewarding. Milton's workmanship is so careful and the story so unified that there is little hope of recognizing, imbedded in the epic, work independently written. Looking at the book of the Creation, the seventh, one can imagine a Biblical paraphrase beginning about line 200, but a poem of 450 lines on such a subject seems unlikely; Du Bartas took more space. The lyrical portions offer more probability. The

were written later than the remaining parts of Books IV-V, Book VI, and apparently sections of Book VIII. . . . As a probability which merits careful consideration, and only as such, I suggest that Milton began composition with sections of Book IV."—*Paradise Lost, An Account of Its Growth and Major Origins, with a Discussion of Milton's Use of Sources and Literary Patterns* (Chicago, 1940), pp. 309, 310, 325.

I do not accept these details as proved, but give them as showing their author's belief in disjunctive composition.

Professor Harris Fletcher writes: Some of the old biographers state that this poem was written piece-

meal, and the more the poem is studied, and the more the reader's conviction grows that such was actually the case."—*The Complete Poetical Works of Milton* (Boston, 1941), p. 153. See also *John Milton's Complete Poetical Works Reproduced in Photographic Facsimile*, ed. Harris Francis Fletcher (Urbana, 1945), II, 9-11.

Dr. Johnson seems to have assumed disjointed composition ("Milton," par. 127, in *Lives of the English Poets* [Oxford, 1905], I, 139).

6. Josephine Waters Bennett, *The Evolution of the Faerie Queene* (Chicago, 1942), pp. 92, 104, 173, 275, 277.

hymn to light beginning Book III might have existed independently.[7]
So may the morning hymn of Adam and Eve (v. 153). In 1648 a
number of Psalms were translated; part of the morning hymn is
founded on Psalm 148. Did Milton write this Biblical lyric only when
he required a hymn for his characters, or did it come from a Psalm
already in English verse?[8] But even though Milton may not have
incorporated any great bulk of material composed for other purposes,
his poem still affords much evidence for composition by the shifting
and insertion of portions both long and short.

The only manuscript of the poem is the fair copy of the first book,[9]
which shows only slight corrections. It differs from the first edition in
many small matters,[10] some of which may be the result of Milton's
proofreading; others may be the work of the printer, accepted by
Milton. A few changes and additions were made in the second edition,
partly in connection with the division of two books to increase the
total number from ten to twelve. Few of these alterations are sig-
nificant for my purpose.[11]

It may be supposed that Milton had the complete manuscript read
aloud to him at least once, perhaps several times. That would have
enabled him to eliminate various seeming duplications that still remain
in the poem.[12] There is, however, no positive evidence for such reading. It may be that Milton—careful workman though he was—

7. Mr. Tillyard (*Milton*, p. 195)
thinks this hymn of about the
date of Milton's *Defensio secunda*,
1654, and considers the similarity
with the passage on blindness
(Columbia ed., VIII, 62-72) evidence for the date of Book III.
The likeness bears on the date of
the hymn itself, but not on the
date of the remainder of Book III,
except as unified composition can
be demonstrated. If Milton did
compose the hymn independently,
he must have revised it to fit its
present place.

8. Such a suggestion is not ruined by
pointing out that the Psalms we
have are not in blank verse.
Ariosto wrote in *terza rima* what

later became a lament in octaves
(*Qual son, qual sempre fui, tal
esser voglio* and *Orlando Furioso*
44.61-66).

9. J. Holly Hanford, "The Manuscript of *Paradise Lost*," *Modern
Philology*, XXV (1928), 313-17.

10. The copies of the first edition
vary among themselves (Masson,
Poetical Works of Milton, London 1903, II, 4). Mr. Harris F.
Fletcher gives the variants in the
second volume of *Milton's
Works Reproduced in Photographic Facsimile* (Urbana,
1945).

11. See the discussion of *capitol-
capital*, Sec. 32, below.

12. See, for example, Sec. 38.

slighted the final synoptic view of his manuscript. That is suggested by the repetitions and inconsistencies now to be found in *Paradise Lost*.[13] It is possible to hold that some of these repetitions are deliberate, and yet to think that the poet failed in a minute adjustment to one another of the various occurrences of a theme.

Milton could hardly have derived a sweeping view of his poem from the proofreading. Though there can hardly be doubt that he had proof sheets, he would not have received at one time the proof of the entire poem or even of some large section of it. Probably he received but eight pages at a time, since the first edition is in quarto form. He would normally have read these eight pages and returned them before he received more proof. Thus the proofreading of the 342 pages of the volume would have been done on forty-three different days, interrupted by Sundays, holidays, and breaks in the routine of printing.[14] So the proofreading would have been of little aid in revealing widely separated inconsistencies so glaring that the poet would have been willing to pay for their correction.

2. Dramatic Plans and Epic Beginnings

MILTON TELLS us that *Paradise Lost* pleased him as a subject for heroic song after "long choosing and beginning late" (IX. 26). But though he had been thinking of epic poetry for many years, we do not know of any interest in the theme of *Paradise Lost* earlier than the plans for

---

13. Lack of final reading also appears, it seems to me, in some of his other works.

14. Milton received his first payment on April 27, 1667, and the volume was entered in the Stationers' Register on August 20, 1667. If the master printer put only one press on the volume, the pressmen probably spent forty-three days in the actual printing of the edition of 1300 copies or a few more. About that number of copies of a sheet was a day's work for two men. See Moxon, *Mechanick* *Exercises*, Sect. 24, No. 21. ¶ 15, ed. De Vinne (New York, 1896), p. 319. See also the editor's note. Mr. Harris F. Fletcher has traced through the first edition of *Paradise Lost* a broken B, which occurs on twenty different pages of the volume, or a little oftener than every second signature from sig. G to the end (*op. cit.*, pp. 280, 294, 316 . . . . 598, 614). Evidently the printer did not have more than two signatures in type at any one time. As soon as possible the type was distributed to be reset.

tragedies in the Cambridge Manuscript.[1] Of these there are four. Three, on the same page, are different states of the same design. The first, which has been crossed out, consists of a list of "the Persons": Michael, Lucifer, Adam and Eve with the serpent, a Chorus of Angels, and a number of allegorical characters. If one may judge from the facsimile of the manuscript, the serpent was an afterthought immediately rejected; at least the word is not written in the column and is independently marked out. Plan Two, also rejected, substitutes Moses for Michael, whose name was first written and then crossed out, omits the serpent, and adds four allegorical characters. Plan Three is entitled *Paradise Lost;* it gives the same list of persons as Plan Two, except for some addition to the mute allegorical figures and the use of an unnamed angel who presents them. It is, however, divided into acts and tells very briefly what is done by the characters, except Heavenly Love and Evening Starre. The prologue, by Moses, is more in detail than any other part but is an obvious addition to what was set down earlier, as though Milton began to expand a plan already in writing but found too little space on the page and paused after enlarging the prologue only.

This intention of giving more detail to his plan is carried out in the fourth draft, written at the bottom of a half-filled page. The title was first *Adams Banishment;* this is canceled and *Adam unparadiz'd* substituted. Though the earlier title of *Paradise Lost* has been abandoned, this draft seemingly is closely related to the third; at any rate there is nothing else extant to which can be applied the words at the end of the fourth: "compare this with the former draught."

1. *Facsimile of the Manuscript of Milton's Minor Poems Preserved in the Library of Trinity College, Cambridge* (ed. William Aldis Wright, Cambridge, 1899). Facsimiles are also given by Harris F. Fletcher, *op. cit.,* II, 12-29, and by Samuel L. Sotheby, *Ramblings in the Elucidation of the Autograph of Milton* (London, 1861), Plates IV-X. See Figs. 1-3 in the present volume, and "Milton's Plan for a Tragedy as Inferred from the Cambridge Manuscript," in this section, below.

For all or part of the plans for tragedies in the manuscript, see the Columbia edition, XVIII, 228-45; *The Student's Milton* (ed. Frank A. Patterson, New York, 1933), pp. 1128-34; *Works of Milton,* ed. Harris Fletcher, pp. 150-52; J. Holly Hanford, *A Milton Handbook* (New York, 1939), pp. 181-86; Grant McColley, *Paradise Lost,* pp. 281-93, and many editions of *Paradise Lost* from the time of Todd to the present.

Both Three and Four now begin with a prologue; in the former Moses is the speaker, in the latter Gabriel. The facsimile of the manuscript shows, however, that the Fourth Plan originally began: "First the chorus," etc. *First* was crossed out and *next* substituted,[2] because, crowded in above, were added directions for the prologue, though that word is not used; it runs: "The angel Gabriel, either descending or entring, shewing since this globe was created, his frequency as much on earth, as in heavn, describes Paradise." The early part of Draft Four is a modification of the first two acts of Draft Three. The debate of Justice, Mercie, and Wisdome in the first act disappears entirely; the Hymn of the Creation closing the first act of the earlier plan is to be retained, for it is mentioned, though not in its proper place,[3] in Plan Four. The second act of Plan Three is very brief, merely naming two characters, Heavenly Love and Evening Starre, and adding: "chorus sing the mariage song and describe Paradice." Heavenly Love and Evening Starre are not named in Draft Four, yet Milton may have intended that Gabriel should mention them when telling of the love and marriage of the first couple. There is no marriage song in Draft Four; indeed there is no place for it. Paradise has already been described by Gabriel in the prologue.

After the second act, Three is much like Four, except that the latter is more detailed. There are two important additions. First, Lucifer himself tells what he has done for the destruction of man; second, an angel informs the chorus of the manner of the Fall. While it is hardly possible that the Fall would not have been narrated in the tragedy entitled *Paradise Lost*, the outline does not clearly show it, as does that for *Adam unparadiz'd*.

Both plans are for dramas with a prologue and with songs by a chorus of angels that remain on the stage throughout the action. In the earlier draft these songs follow the acts; the later draft is not divided into acts, but apparently the intention was the same. Indeed Milton, having forgotten to indicate in the last draft the first of these choric songs, writes, as though at the end of the second act: "as before

2. J. Milton French, "Chips from Milton's Workshop," *ELH*, X (1943), 239.
3. As appears in Milton's Plan for a Tragedy (below in this section)

this hymn is mentioned at the end of Act II, though intended for the end of Act I. See also Fig. 2.

after the first act was sung a hymn of the creation."[4] He had some further difficulty in remembering his choruses; in the last draft two of them are written below the body of the outline, with indication where they are to be inserted.

If it is proper to take at full value Milton's direction to compare the last "with the former draught," his complete intention may be arrived at by combining the two, with the omission of whatever in the third is superseded by something in the last.

In the following, items derived from the third plan are in italics, items to be omitted are in angular brackets, additions are in square brackets.[5]

MILTON'S PLAN FOR A TRAGEDY AS INFERRED FROM
THE CAMBRIDGE MANUSCRIPT

Adam unparadiz'd

[Prologue][6]

The angel Gabriel, either descending or entring, shewing since this globe was created, his frequency as much on earth, as in heavn, describes Paradise.

[Act 1]

next the Chorus [of Angels] shewing the reason of his[7] coming to keep his watch in Paradise after Lucifers rebellion by command from

4. It seems that *before* can hardly be taken to mean in "the former draught," to wit, the third, though there the "hymn of the creation" is indicated at the end of act one.
5. This scheme differs in some particulars from that of Francis Peck in *New Memoirs of the Life and Poetical Works of Mr. John Milton* (London, 1740), pp. 40-41, and from that of Mr. McColley, *Paradise Lost*, pp. 286-88. For the original, see Figs. 1, 2, and 3.
6. The word *prologue* (in Greek) appears in the third draft, though

not in the fourth. Peck and Mc-Colley put Gabriel in the first act.
7. *His* in this quotation refers to the Chorus, not to Gabriel. Milton frequently uses a singular verb with *Chorus*, though nowhere else a singular pronoun (few pronouns occur). The manuscript makes the reference plain. As has been said, Gabriel was a late addition, so that when the draft was first written there was no noun except *chorus* to which the pronouns could refer. See Fig. 2.

god, & withall expressing his desire to see, & know more concerning this excellent new creature man.[8] the angel Gabriel as by his name signifying a prince of power tracing paradise with a more free office passes by the station of the chorus & desired by them relates what he knew of man as the creation of Eve with thire love, & mariage.

[Chorus]

Chorus of Angels sing a hymne of the creation.[9]

Act 2

after this Lucifer appeares after his overthrow, bemoans himself, seeks revenge on man   the Chorus prepare resistance at his first approach   at last after discourse of enmity on either side he departs

[Chorus]

whereat the chorus sings of the battell, & victorie in heavn against him, & his accomplices, {as before after the first act was sung a hymn of the creation}

Act 3

heer again may appear Lucifer relating, & insulting in what he had don to the destruction of man.   man next & Eve having by this time bin seduc't by the serpent appeares confusedly cover'd with leaves conscience in a shape accuses him, Justice cites him to the place whither Jehova call'd for him   in the mean while the chorus entertains the stage, & is inform'd by some angel the manner of his fall

[Chorus]

heer the chorus bewailes Adams fall.

8. McColley ends the first act here. It seems, however, unlikely that an act would be given to the chorus alone or even to Gabriel's first speech plus a soliloquy by the chorus, for apparently Gabriel, if he remains on the stage, does not converse with them until he passes by their station. A hymn of the Creation by the chorus is more suitable after Gabriel has told of man and the creation of Eve than it is when the chorus has merely expressed a desire to know.

9. Incidentally, to put here the hymn of creation introduces early in *Adam unparadiz'd* the matter of the seventh book of *Paradise Lost*, thus breaking the sequence indicated by McColley (*Paradise Lost*, p. 293), but the break is not enough to invalidate his statement that *Adam unparadiz'd* is on the whole in the sequence of the epic.

Act 4[10]

Adam then & Eve returne accuse one another but especially Adam layes the blame to his wife, is stubborn in his offence   Justice appeares reason[s] with him convinces him

[Chorus]

the chorus admonisheth Adam, & bids him beware by Lucifers example of impenitence

[Act 5]

the Angel is sent to banish them out of paradise but before causes to passe before his eyes in Shapes a mask of all the evills *Labour, greife, hatred, Envie, warre, famine, Pestilence, sicknesse, discontent, Ignorance, Feare, Death, winter, heat, Tempest, &c.*   of this life & world he is humbl'd relents, dispaires,   at last appears Mercy   comforts him   promises the Messiah, then calls in faith, hope, & charity, instructs him he repents gives god the glory submits to his penalty

[Chorus]

the chorus briefly concludes.
{compare this with the former draught.}

In addition to the plans outlined in the manuscript, we know of a fifth plan: [11] Edward Phillips writes that the subject of the Fall of man "was first designed a Tragedy, and in the Fourth Book of the Poem there are Ten Verses, which several Years before the Poem was begun, were shown to me, and some others, as designed for the very beginning of the said Tragedy."[12] He then quotes, with "glorious" instead of "matchless" in the last line, *Paradise Lost* IV. 32-41. It seems

---

10. Here McColley begins the fifth act. A reason in support is that, so far as the outline indicates, Adam and Eve do not hereafter leave the stage. This makes a very long act. In support of division is the appearance of the chorus, but they appear to speak directly to Adam rather than to sing a hymn as after the other acts. In Draft Three the last act is entirely occupied with the mask of the evils they are to suffer and with the comfort given by the virtues. The fourth plan, however, contains matter not mentioned in Three. My inclination is toward the order indicated by the mention of the chorus. It is that adopted by Peck (*loc. cit.*).

11. Grant McColley, "Milton's Lost Tragedy," *Philological Quarterly*, XVIII (1939), 78-83.

12. *Life of Milton*, in Darbishire, *Early Lives of Milton*, p. 72.

likely that the difference is Phillips' error. "Glorious" occurs a few lines before and its repetition here is not according to Milton's habits of echoing words. Satan's address to the Sun in *Paradise Lost* iv. 32-41 could not have been the beginning of a formal prologue like that of the tragedy just outlined. It is rather a plunge directly into the action, more violent than that beginning *Samson Agonistes*. Yet Phillips, on whom all our knowledge depends, says that the lines were "designed for the very beginning of the said tragedy." Unless we reject his testimony, we must infer that the fifth plan was for a drama much different, in its beginning at least, from those outlined in the Cambridge Manuscript. Did this difference extend throughout the play? Whether anything more than the ten lines that Phillips quotes was written according to the fifth plan there is no evidence.[13] Considering Milton's interest in the subject over many years, it is hard to believe that he had not produced a good deal of manuscript. Is it not likely that in the "several years" between Phillips' sight of the ten lines and Milton's first work on the epic, much of the tragedy, or even all of it, was written according to the fifth plan? But we can only infer. Phillips, though he "had the perusal" of *Paradise Lost* "from the very beginning" as "from time to time" he went to visit his uncle,[14] says nothing of the use of further lines from a work earlier than the poem; in fact his account suggests new composition altogether, save these few verses. Doubtless the fifth plan was later than four.[15] At least if the fourth plan

13. In *A Preface to Paradise Lost* (Oxford, 1942), Mr. C. S. Lewis comments on "and add thy name O Sun" (iv. 36-37): "On the stage Satan would have had to do this in order to let the audience know whom he was addressing. Would Milton have inserted these words if the passage had been originally epic, not dramatic?"—P. 134. Also on

> Of these the vigilance
> I dread, and to elude, thus wrapt
>   in mist
> Of midnight vapor glide obscure,
>   and prie

In every Bush and Brake, where hap may finde
The Serpent sleeping
                           (ix. 157-61)

he comments: "These four lines sound very much as if they had been originally written for the stage."—P. 135.

Peck writes: "I cannot help thinking that, beside the bare plans, he also wrote a good deal of the Drama itself (perhaps all)."—*New Memoirs . . . of Milton*, p. 37.

14. Darbishire, *Early Lives*, p. 73.
15. McColley, *Paradise Lost*, pp. 291, 301.

is altered by putting at the beginning Satan, now mentioned about one-third of the way through, its order of events is much like that of the epic.[16]

Does the epic itself furnish any evidence on the nature of this tragedy according to the fifth plan? This question should rather be put in the form: What parts of *Paradise Lost* may once have been included in a drama?[17]

Since the setting of such a work must have been the Garden of Eden, the first book, with its scene in Hell and its catalogue of the followers of Satan, is not possible for Milton's stage. The same is true of the second book, with its council and Satan's great voyage. Parts of these books might have been employed in some other form, as in a soliloquy by Satan when he "seeks revenge upon man" (Plan Four), or may have been alluded to on the stage, but could not have been otherwise used.

The early part of the third book is so important for the idea of *Paradise Lost* that a less developed counterpart of it probably appeared in the drama, as when Justice, Mercy, and Wisdom debate "what should become of man if he fall" (Plan Three, Act I), or when Messiah is promised (Plan Four). Satan's pretended desire to know more of man (III. 662) is that of the Chorus early in Plan Four. Lines 383-99 are perhaps from the choric song of "the battell, & victorie in heavn against him, & his accomplices" planned for Draft Four.

The fourth book has much affinity with tragedy. Its scene is the Garden. Satan's first speech (IV. 32-113) is a soliloquy including the lines Phillips says Milton wrote for Plan Five. This passage and others (IV. 360-91, 504-35) show "Lucifer contriving Adam's ruin" as in Plan Three, Act III, and bemoaning himself and seeking revenge on

---

16. This has been worked out by McColley (*Paradise Lost*, pp. 292-93). It seems that the words "expressing his desire to see, & know more concerning this excellent new creature man" are parallel to III. 661-80, 696-735 and that these passages might have been indicated on page 292. They do not, however, cause an important break in sequence.

17. Peck writes: "If it be true . . .

that besides the bare plans, our author likewise wrote a good deal of the drama itself (perhaps all) and then took it to pieces and inserted the main of it into [*Paradise Lost*], then, with the help of the plans which he hath left us, it were easie to throw the Paradise Lost back again into a dramatic poem."— *Op. cit.*, p. 41.

man as in Plan Four. A considerable part of the book describes Paradise (iv. 132 ff., 543 ff., etc.); so does the Chorus in Plan Three, Act II, and Gabriel in Plan Four. The Evening Star is alluded to (iv. 605) as in Plans Two and Three, Act II, and the marriage song (iv. 710-18, 741-70) as in Plan Three, Act II; the love and marriage of Adam and Eve is dealt with in Plan Four. As the angelic guardians prepare to fight with Satan but let him escape (iv. 782-1013; cf. also line 684), so in Plan Four the Chorus prepare to resist him, and "after discourse of enmity" he departs. There are soliloquies by Satan other than his first one, and conversation by the human actors (iv. 411-91, 610-88). The evening prayer is suited for drama (iv. 720-35). The spoken lines of the book run to four hundred; a play would have had stage directions in addition, and perhaps some of the other material would have been worked into dialogue.

Part of the fifth book may also have been included in a drama. Dialogue between Adam and Eve occupies lines 28-128, and their morning prayer, perhaps not originally in their mouths,[18] is also suitable for tragedy (v. 153-208). Conversation about and with Raphael takes some 215 lines more. The remainder of the book is given to his narrative of the War in Heaven. This could have appeared in drama in abbreviated form: in Plan Three, Act III, the Chorus relates Lucifer's rebellion and fall, and in Plan Four it sings of the battle and victory in Heaven. The portions of Book V in dialogue and prayer amount to some 370 lines.

Some of the matter of the sixth book would have been included in the chorus just mentioned, except for the angel's warning at the end (vi. 900-12), which might have been in Plan Five.

As a whole the seventh book is impossible for tragedy, but the forty lines of its hymn of Creation (vii. 565-73, 602-32) are such as are indicated for Plan Three, Act I, and for Plan Four.

The eighth book is primarily dialogue. Yet it seems unlikely that a drama could have contained its astronomical discussion. The account of Adam's creation, which he relates to the angel, might have been intended for action on the stage, with the dialogue between Adam and his Maker actually spoken instead of reported—provided Milton, like Andreini, was willing to present the Almighty as an actor. It

18. See Sec. 1.

should be noticed, however, that the fourth plan has Justice cite Adam "to the place whither Jehova call'd for him   in the mean while the chorus entertains the stage;" the Judgment takes place off the stage and the Judge does not appear. So probably Jehovah did not have a part in any dramatic predecessor of Book VIII. Adam's enthusiastic praise of Eve and his rebuke by the angel presumably would have been spoken on the boards. Here also is a hint of the marriage song (VIII. 519), partly given in Book IV, sung according to Plans Three and Four. Adam's description of his "pleaded reason" to Eve suggests dramatic action. Much of this might have appeared, without being acted out, in such tragedies as Milton outlined. For example in Plan Four he arranged that Gabriel should relate the "creation of Eve with thire love, & mariage." In Book VIII as it now stands, the dialogue that may well have been part of the tragedy according to Plan Five amounts only to some 240 lines.

The ninth book is primarily dramatic. A considerable part of it, however, is given to stage setting, not all of which could have been incorporated in the text of a play however descriptive. Soliloquy and dialogue run to almost nine hundred lines. In the fourth plan some angel tells "the manner of [Adam's] fall." In that plan also Adam and Eve accuse one another and Adam blames his wife, as in IX. 1134-89, and in the Argument, which speaks of their "variance and accusation of one another."

The tenth book in part continues the dramatic character of the preceding one and in part deals with such wholly epic matters as the announcement of the Fall in Heaven, the bridge of Sin and Death, and the council in Hell. Perhaps this epic part owes something to Plan Four, in which Milton inserted, writing on the opposite page, the words: "heer again may appear Lucifer relating, & insulting in what he had don to the destruction of man." Is this the germ of Satan's speech in triumph, especially of

> Him by fraud I have seduc'd
> From his Creator, and the more to increase
> Your wonder, with an Apple; he thereat
> Offended, worth your laughter, hath giv'n up
> Both his beloved Man and all his World,
> To Sin and Death a prey.   (x. 485-90)

Dialogue and the like in the Garden run to about 450 lines, of which
121 are occupied by Adam's soliloquy, the longest speech in the poem
except the formal narratives of the angels. The judgment by the Son
(x. 96-208) suggests the entry in Plan Three, Act IV: "Conscience
cites them to Gods Examination." Plan Four reads: "Justice cites him
to the place whither Jehova call'd for him. . . . Adam then & Eve
returne accuse one another but especially Adam layes the blame to
his wife, is stubborn in his offence." This blaming of Eve appears in
the epic both at the Judgment and later. Since, according to Draft IV,
the guilty ones are called off the stage for judgment, the Judge does
not appear. The "winter, heat Tempest" of Plan Three, Act V, are
developed into the change of climate after the Fall (x. 651-706, 846-51,
1062-69).

The early part of book eleven has conversation between Adam,
Eve, and Michael running to almost 190 lines. The "good Adam
hath lost" of Plan Three, Act IV, appears in xi. 58-59, 271-81. The
eleventh and twelfth books present the ills which appear as mutes in
Plan Three, Act V, and in the mask of evils in Plan Four.

In the twelfth book there are at present some seventy-five lines
in dialogue. Michael's instruction of Adam is parallel to the comfort
and teaching by Faith, Hope, and Charity in Plan Three, Act V, and
to the work of Mercy in Plan Four, where she promises the Messiah,
calls in the three virtues, and instructs Adam. He repents, gives God
the glory, and submits, as in xii. 552-73.

Paradise Lost contains, then, a large amount of dialogue, much
of which is so combined with action as to seem suited for drama.
If anything may be inferred from this, it is that Satan's vigorous
soliloquy in the opening lines according to Plan Five set the tone for
the whole. In the early plans much is spoken by the Chorus, but in
the fifth plan the choric speeches would have been less important than
earlier, perhaps not more prominent than in Jonson's *Catiline*, and
there would have been less narration and more action and dialogue.
It is hardly to be supposed that all the dialogue of the present epic is
derived from the drama, if only because that dialogue runs to some
2,700 lines, nearly a thousand lines longer than *Samson Agonistes*.[19]

19. For a different attempt to estimate the length of the tragedy, see Sec. 51,
below.

The tragedy of *Paradise Lost* is not on the Greek model, but on one much less limited,[20] yet there is no reason to suppose that it would have been a very long work. Other material, in addition to dialogue, such as description of Paradise and choric songs, would have added considerably to the length based on conversation alone.

Among the pieces of epic dialogue that may not have appeared in the tragedy mentioned by Phillips is one of much importance, namely the discourse of Satan and Eve in Book IX. That book contains far more conversation, as distinct from narrative, than any other in the epic, but in the second, third, and fourth plans for dramas its main action is not put on the stage; in Plan Four an angel tells "the manner of his fall," briefly it seems. With all the art possible in developing a narrator's function, Milton could hardly have secured through a messenger the effect of the action of Book IX. Indeed to write a dramatic *Paradise Lost* without showing the taking of the fruit seems like playing all around the main action without actually touching it. Apparently Milton intended to dramatize that deed when in Plan One he listed among the persons "Adam [and] Eve with the serpent." Why did he abandon the serpent? Was he thinking of the stage and unwilling to repeat the effect of the disguised Satan in Andreini's *Adamo?*[21] If Satan is Milton's Iago, could he have appeared on the stage in the form of "the wily adder," however lovely, to converse with Eve? Would all the fables of Jove in serpent form (IX. 508), all the paintings of the Temptation, all the respect of the age for Biblical story have led Milton to give one of his most important speaking parts to a snake? After the first canceled draft, the serpent is not one of "the persons." If he did not reappear in the fifth plan, Milton may have felt that omission of the crucial scene was ruinous, and therefore have abandoned the tragedy. It may be, however, that in the last plan the serpent did again come on the stage. If so, Milton's feeling against an

20. William R. Parker, "The Trinity Manuscript and Milton's Plans for a Tragedy," *JEGP*, XXXIV (1935), 230. The plans in the Cambridge Manuscript indicate allegorical characters for *Paradise Lost* only. Some of the other dramas, as *Sodom,* are also evidently more elaborate than *Samson Agonistes. Abias Thersaeus* is, however, much of the same sort. The name of this tragedy means *Abijah at Tirzah,* not, as the Columbia edition (XVIII, 237) has it, *Sought for.*

21. It seems unlikely that Milton saw *Adamo* performed. It is possible that he read the play.

animal actor may have been among the reasons that led him to abandon tragedy for epic,[22] in which the disguised Tempter could play his part with dignity.

If the drama according to Plan Five did not show Eve's temptation, it can hardly have been, according to Elizabethan standards, excessively long. The opening lines by Satan of which Edward Phillips tells allow of a play with many Elizabethan qualities,[23] as appears in the segregation earlier in this section of the dramatic passages of the epic; especially Elizabethan is the masque. Yet the drama would probably have been more classical than Jonson's *Catiline*. Ben does not hold strictly to the city of Rome, but John's fourth plan limits the action to the Garden.[24]

Having, then, a tragedy planned and perhaps wholly written, Milton's problem was to transform it into an epic. First he needed to change stage directions into descriptive verse and to supplement and enlarge references to setting. Much stage action also now had to be narrated. Then there were parts appearing in Plan Four and perhaps also in Plan Five that needed to be reconsidered and, if they were already on paper, to be rewritten and expanded. The battle in Heaven and Satan's overthrow, represented only by choric song, had to become narrative. The "hymn of the creation," perhaps much like the hymn at the end of the seventh book, had to be supplied with supporting description. The "mask of all the evills of this life" was quite changed, to become in part the representative narratives from Genesis in Book XI and in part the general view of history in Book XII. Something of the original plan was thus given up, since there seems no intention to indicate evils in the accounts of Jubal and Tubal-cain, and the Old Testament history, though showing the idolatry of Israel, does not attempt to cover the list of evils in Plan Three; indeed a number of these evils

22. The larger reasons for Milton's shift from the tragic to the epic form of *Paradise Lost* are not for this volume. Had he, when he made the change, decided that epic rather than tragedy is "the gravest, moralest, and most profitable of all other poems"?— Preface to *Samson Agonistes*.

23. J. Holly Hanford, "The Dramatic Element in *Paradise Lost*," *Studies in Philology*, XIV (1917), 178-95.

24. I suspect that the third plan does also, though the words "Adam and Eve, driven out of Paradice praesented by an angel with Labour," etc., might mean that they saw the mutes after leaving the Garden.

do not specifically appear in the poem as it now stands. Milton had, however, as the other plans in the Cambridge Manuscript show, given thought to the tragic possibilities of early Biblical narratives other than the story of Adam and Eve, since there are such titles as *The flood, The Deluge, Abram in Egypt, Josuah in Gibeon*. Some of these, like *Dagonalia*, which became *Samson Agonistes*,[25] may have been written out; Noah's flood receives a good deal of attention in Book XI.

In addition to transforming his old material, Milton was obliged to devise new scenes fitted for epic, especially those in Hell, Chaos, and Heaven. They must be added to a plot already complete. The War in Heaven presents a rebellion in various respects similar to that of man, though contrasted in that Satan and his host

> by thir own suggestion fell,
> Self-tempted, self-deprav'd: man falls deceiv'd
> By the other first.   (III. 129-31)

It shows by means of his earlier deeds the character of Satan, the villain of the tragedy. The War in Heaven is hence so important that it was the subject of a choric song in Plan Four, which perhaps developed Satan as a worthy adversary. Still his rebellion is not part of the plot of a drama called *Adams Banishment* or *Adam unparadiz'd*. The struggle in Heaven decides nothing about man. The only one of the rebellious army who is later to take part in the action is the leader himself.

What has been said of the War in Heaven applies also to the debates in Hell in Books I and II, with the difference that the latter result in action against far-distant man, but so many are the verses dominated by Satan that man's affairs are overwhelmed. Again many of the actors step forth only for the moment. Satan's host is impressive as its roll is called, but that host is not going forth to battle. Its military feats are in the past. The poet says that Moloc and Dagon and the others are in the future to appear on earth as enemies of man, but they take no further part; they are arrayed for epic display, not for action.

25. There is reason to suspect that *Samson Agonistes* is earlier in date than the time of its publication indicates. Edward Phil-lips says he did not know when it was written (*Life of Milton*, in Darbishire, *Early Lives*, p. 75).

Likewise the council in Book II is overlong for the purpose of starting Satan on his mission, and is ornamental rather than vital, resulting in deeds only by Satan, not by his followers; even the plan determined on was devised by the leader himself, and did not come out of the debate. The voyage, though a fine epic spectacle, is also not essential; in the tragedy, Satan had to get to the Garden without it. Sin and Death, unlike other highly characterized enemies of God and man, do appear once more, yet even they are not shown actually at work in the world. All of these scenes in Heaven and Hell because of which Satan has been thought the hero of *Paradise Lost* are additions to the original tragic basis.

The first half of Book III presents characters of the utmost importance. The Godhead is always before the minds' eyes of Milton's characters, whether in Hell, on Earth, or in Heaven. The ideas of the book are of vast importance to the poet. God's mercy and justice, foreknowledge, free will—these are the matters that as a religious teacher he wished to expound, and in Book III they are set forth as by no other poet. Yet even for *Paradise Lost* they are not unique ideas; the eleventh and twelfth books give them all, less strikingly it is true. Though the verses in themselves are extraordinary, nothing would be lacking in plot and idea if the theological part of Book III were not there. The function of that book is to contribute to the spectacular effect of the epic by cutting off and ruining Satan before ever he reaches the Garden, so that all he does is vain.

Book VII is also an epic spectacle. In the dramas there could be no long narrative of Creation, as distinct from a hymn. The seventh book is less necessary to the action than any other considerable part of the poem; indeed this "Hexameron" is like a highly concentrated form of Du Bartas' *Divine Weeks and Works* introduced for its own sake and for the variety it gives rather than for any other reason; yet for a poet later than Du Bartas who was dealing at length with the early part of Genesis nothing could be more natural; this was especially true of Milton who, *anno aetatis* 19, wrote in his poem *At a Vacation Exercise* that he hoped to

> sing of secret things that came to pass
> When Beldam Nature in her cradle was.

One may say, then, that Milton took a play and made it into a heroic poem by adding half-extraneous material. The new parts, vital to *Paradise Lost* as we now have it, are not vital to the story of man's Fall. The parts relating to Satan are not part of the primary plot but form a subplot. The angel's narrative is called the episode of the poem but differs from the episodes in the *Odyssey* and the *Aeneid*. Their narrators are the chief actors of the poem and they tell their own adventures. The narrator of *Paradise Lost* is brought in that he may tell the story and insists on the illustrative importance of his matter:

> Let it profit thee to have heard
> By terrible Example the reward
> Of disobedience.   (VI. 909-11)

It also furnishes a parallel to the Fall of man. These functions of the War in Heaven are more evident than is its lengthening of the central story—the primary purpose of the classical episode. Milton's episode lies between the narrative of Aeneas and the tale of Ariosto's innkeeper, who by telling of Fiammetta illustrates Rodomonte's theme of female inconstancy. Milton's art of composition made all the added parts indispensable to his epic, but that epic differs from other epics in that it is still at heart a tragedy. Indeed, even though in the seventeenth century the theological view of Adam's fall, with its implications for the human race, gave it a universal quality such as we now hardly feel, Milton was in a narrow literary sense more nearly right when he thought of *Paradise Lost* as a drama than when he made it into what is called an epic. We may be thankful that he did not shrink from bombasting his tragedy with scenes in Hell and Heaven. A happy thing it is that he consulted his own genius, or what he called "blameless nature," to the "inriching of art." A drama of *Paradise Lost* or a heroic poem on King Arthur or King Alfred would have been a noble work, but would not have exhibited Milton's use of variety or drawn on his creative powers to give poetry something new as did the inspired choice he made.

CHAPTER TWO

THE OUTLINE OF *PARADISE LOST*

IT MAY now be asked what reason the details of the poem offer for belief in composition other than by steady movement from the first line to the last. Such reason is to be found largely in departures from harmony between the parts. In this and later chapters are noted all the inconsistencies that have been observed, with any hints they give on order of composition. Sometimes, however, it has been impossible to do more than point out the seeming break in the pattern.

3. The Arguments

S. SIMMONS, the printer of the first edition of *Paradise Lost*, says in a note to the reader : "There was no argument at first intended to the Book, but for the satisfaction of many that have desired it, I have procur'd it." What was this argument that the printer procured? Did Milton on getting Simmons' request set to work afresh, or did he have among his papers something that with a little revision was suitable? Was there an outline he had followed in composing that he could easily turn into an argument? It can hardly be doubted that he had a "draught," like those in the Cambridge Manuscript, used as a guide during his years of labor; if it was to serve its purpose it must have been changed when he made changes in plan. The earliest outline for the epic presumably was made with the plans for the drama of *Paradise Lost* in mind. There are even a few similarities in wording:

Argument, Book IV: he . . . prepares resistance
Draft Four: the Chorus prepare resistance [Note the change of
    person.]

Argument, Book IX: they . . . fall to variance and accusation of one
    another.
Draft Four: Adam and Eve . . . accuse one another

Argument, Book X: Satan . . . relates with boasting his success against
    Man.
Draft Four: Lucifer relating and insulting in what he had don to the
    destruction of man.

Besides this, the arguments and the plans for dramas are similar in
manner. The form is that of notes for the author's own use rather than
of prose addressed to an audience. One of the similarities is the omission
of conjunctions between clauses. The outlines are written contin-
uously and so for the most part are the arguments, though in the latter
topics are sometimes merely announced, as in that of Book IV: "thir
Bower describ'd; thir Evening worship." Such announcement occurs
more easily in the argument of an epic,[1] with its opportunity for description, than in a drama, which more specifically represents men in
action; these changes might show revision of the outline before it was
sent to the printer as an argument. But even though Milton revised
his outline, did he make it exactly fit the present state of the poem?
    According to the Argument of Book I, Satan was "by the com-
mand of God driven out of Heaven with all his Crew into the great
Deep." This fits the orders to Gabriel and Michael before their combat with the rebels (VI. 44-55), and echoes the word *deep* in the commission, hardly a command, given to the Son before he expelled
Satan from Heaven (VI. 710-16). But the text of Book I does not
represent Satan as fighting against the angels or the Son; his attempt
is against the Most High, the Omnipotent, and

> Him the Almighty Power
> Hurld headlong flaming from th'Ethereal Skie.   (I. 44-5)

These lines tell of direct action by the Godhead, not commands to
angels.[2] The Argument of Book I reads: "To find out the truth of
this Prophesie, and what to determin thereon he [Satan] refers to a
full Councell," and the rebel leader says:

---

1. Cf. the arguments of Cowley's
    Davideis.
2. See Sec. 17, below. To be sure,

the Almighty's power can be
made to include the angels.

> These thoughts
> Full Counsel must mature. (I. 659-60)

Yet there is no immediate discussion of the prophecy by a council of
devils. *Refers to* means *brings before* and that is not done until Book II.
The argument continues: "What his Associates thence attempt." I find
nothing in the poem to justify this. After Satan's speech, his followers
draw their swords, rage against the Highest, and hurl defiance toward
the vault of heaven. This is hardly attempting something. The Argument then goes on to the building of Pandaemonium, related in full
in the poem, and continues: "The infernal Peers there sit in Councel."
This, the council to which much of the next book is devoted, is not
the same as that earlier mentioned in the Argument; that seems to have
been concluded and something attempted as the result of it. Since
Milton would hardly have presented two councils in succession, the
second seems a later-devised substitute for the first. At least the Argument seems to speak of two councils; the completed poem tells of
but one.

The Argument for Book II says that "Satan debates whether
another Battel be to be hazarded for the recovery of Heaven." His
speech hardly does that, though he says:

> We now return
> To claim our just inheritance of old,
> . . . . . and by what best way,
> Whether of open Warr or covert guile,
> We now debate. (II. 37 ff.)

The Argument is exceedingly brief for the speeches of Moloc,
Belial, and Mammon, being merely: "some advise it, others dissuade."[3]
Such brevity, though it proves nothing, does suggest that the passage
was written before the characters and their speeches were so fully
developed as now. The summary of Book III gives as much to some
fifty-five verses on the various persons later to be found in the Paradise
of Fools: "What persons and things fly up thither." Though there are
some exceptions,[4] the Arguments usually not only represent the text

3. Similarly in the argument of *Samson Agonistes* the visits of Dalila and Harapha are indicated

only by saying that he "is visited by other persons."

4. Sin and Death are not named in

correctly but are proportioned to it in length. The summary of Book II
then continues: "A third proposal is prefer'd, mention'd before by
Satan, to search the truth of that Prophesie or Tradition in Heaven
concerning another world." This suggests the Argument of Book I:
"To find out the truth of this Prophesie . . . he refers to a full Councell." The summary soon continues: "Thir doubt who shall be sent
on this difficult search." *Doubt* suggests some debate on the matter,
though there is none; they do show dismay at the danger. The next
puzzle is the statement: "He passes on his Journey to Hell Gates, finds
them shut, and who sat there to guard them, by whom at length they
are op'nd." It is curious that Sin and Death are not named, though in
the poem they are dealt with in more detail than is Chaos, who is
named. Were they devised later than the summary?[5]

The Argument of Book III, the second longest, gives with ac-
curacy the contents of the book, except that it disregards the first fifty-
five lines, on blindness.

The Argument to Book IV says that Gabriel "appoints two strong
Angels to Adams Bower, least the evill spirit should be there doing
some harm to Adam or Eve sleeping; there they find him at the ear of
Eve, tempting her in a dream." The actual charge is less specific than
in the summary, and includes the entire garden:

> Ithuriel and Zephon, with wingd speed
> Search through this Garden, leave unsearcht no nook,
> But chiefly where those two fair Creatures Lodge,
> Now laid perhaps asleep secure of harme.   (IV. 788-91)

In the verse Satan is not said to be actually tempting Eve; he is striving
to reach the organs of her fancy, that he might forge phantasms and
dreams, and taint her animal spirits.

In the Argument of Book V, we read that "God . . . sends Raphael
to admonish him of his obedience, of his free estate, of his enemy near

---

the Argument of Book II, nor is
the Son mentioned as the "occasion" of Satan's revolt (Bk. II,
Arg.). The failure to tell of each
of the Six Days of Creation in
the Argument of Book VII probably only indicates that Milton
felt them too well known to

require individual treatment.

It may be observed that the
three exceptions to full statement
relate to passages that for other
reasons are thought to have appeared late in the poem (see
Secs. 14, 31, 38, below).

5. See Sec. 38, below.

at hand." The text develops this message in ten lines; such brevity is not strange, for the points—earlier developed—need to be little more than named. Somewhat further in the Argument it is said that "Raphael performs his message, minds Adam of his state and of his enemy." This refers to a passage in which the angel does speak of obedience and of free will, but alludes to Satan only thus:

> And some are fall'n, to disobedience fall'n,
> And so from Heav'n to deepest Hell.   (v. 541-2)

There is here no suggestion that the fallen ones—unknown to Adam— are enemies of man. That is made clear only at the end of the next book:

> To thee I have reveal'd
> . . . . the deep fall
> Of those too high aspiring, who rebelld
> With Satan, hee who envies now thy state,
> Who now is plotting how he may seduce
> Thee also from obedience, that with him
> Bereavd of happiness thou maist partake
> His punishment, Eternal miserie;
> Which would be all his solace and revenge,
> As a despite don against the most High,
> Thee once to gaine Companion of his woe.   (VI. 895-907)

According to the Argument of Book V, this passage should follow line 542 of that book. The Argument of Book VI wholly disregards it, concluding with the matter of the paragraph preceding that on the enemy: "Messiah returns with triumph to his Father." Apparently when these arguments were written the warning against the enemy was in the fifth book rather than in the sixth.[6]

Except that the Arguments for Books VII and IX do not notice the autobiographical introductions, the only succeeding argument that offers difficulty is that of Book X. It runs: "Sin and Death . . . feeling the success of Satan in this new World, and the sin by Man there committed, resolve to . . . follow Satan thir Sire up to the place of Man." In the text there is no indication that they feel the sin of Man; they do feel Satan's success.

6. See Sec. 19, below.

It appears, then, that there are instances in which the Argument was not written directly from the finished poem but leaves an important portion little represented or gives not quite what the verses say. Moreover, if the outline were wholly later than the poem, would not the introductory lines of Books III, VII, and IX have been included, with those of Book I? Is it possible that the three autobiographical introductions were omitted as not part of the narrative? Unless this is true, it seems that the Arguments represent not the latest state of the poem but one before the introductory lines of the three books were planned. Altogether the effect is that parts of the Arguments are earlier than the final form of the poem itself.

CHAPTER THREE

PASSAGES INFLUENCED BY THE TRAGEDIES

4. Noah and the Flood
(XI. 719-53, 808-29)

AFTER MICHAEL has shown Adam a bloody scene of warfare, with appropriate comment, he presents man living in the licentiousness of peace, which leads to civil war; then

> At length a Reverend Sire among them came,
> And of thir doings great dislike declar'd,
> And testifi'd against thir ways; hee oft
> Frequented thir Assemblies, whereso met,
> Triumphs or Festivals, and to them preachd
> Conversion and Repentance, as to Souls
> In Prison under Judgements imminent:
> But all in vain. (XI. 719-26)

Withdrawing from mankind, he prepares the Ark, which, with its passengers and freight, is described in ten lines, followed by an account of the Flood itself. Adam bewails the fate of his children and asks whether this is the end of the race of men. Michael explains the transition from the violence of war to the luxury of peace on the part of the conquerors and the loss of virtue by the conquered, so that all men are "degenerate,"

> One Man except, the onely Son of light
> In a dark Age, against example good,
> Against allurement, custom, and a World
> Offended; fearless of reproach and scorn,
> Or violence, hee of thir wicked wayes

> Shall them admonish, and before them set
> The paths of righteousness, how much more safe,
> And full of peace, denouncing wrauth to come
> On thir impenitence; and shall returne
> Of them derided, but of God observd
> The one just Man alive; by his command
> Shall build a wondrous Ark, as thou beheldst.   (xi. 808-19)

Since Adam's question sprang from his view of the Ark on the waves, it is strange that the story of Noah is thus a second time introduced as though it were unknown, with no reference to the account already given until the last line quoted. The angel then gives a different version of the Flood itself, and continues with the new material of the subsidence of the waters.

The first account of the storm and the rise of the waters is as follows:

> Meanwhile the Southwind rose, and with black wings
> Wide hovering, all the Clouds together drove
> From under Heav'n; the Hills to their supplie
> Vapour, and Exhalation dusk and moist,
> Sent up amain; and now the thick'nd Skie
> Like a dark Ceeling stood; down rush'd the Rain
> Impetuous, and continu'd till the Earth
> No more was seen; the floating Vessel swum
> Uplifted; and secure with beaked prow
> Rode tilting o're the Waves, all dwellings else
> Flood overwhelmd, and them with all thir pomp
> Deep under water rould; Sea cover'd Sea,
> Sea without shoar; and in thir Palaces
> Where luxurie late reign'd, Sea-monsters whelp'd
> And stabl'd; of Mankind, so numerous late,
> All left, in one small bottom swum imbark't.   (xi. 738-53)

The second description is briefer:

> All the Cataracts
> Of Heav'n set open on the Earth shall powre
> Raine day and night, all fountains of the Deep
> Broke up, shall heave the Ocean to usurp

> Beyond all bounds, till inundation rise
> Above the highest Hills.   (XI. 824-29)

This is more Biblical than the earlier passage, echoing "The same day were all the fountains of the great deep broken up, and the windows of heaven were opened" (Gen. 7:11). These clauses are not found in the first description, though the counterparts of both come in the account, taken from Gen. 8:2, of the drying up of the Flood:

> . . . . the deep, who now had stopt
> His Sluces, as the Heav'n his windows shut.   (XI. 848-49)

But though the less Biblical account of the rise and spread of the waters is with its rhetorical detail longer than the second one, the first account of Noah's preaching is rather more Biblical and somewhat shorter, though still elaborated with the hardly Biblical

> Frequented thir Assemblies, whereso met,
> Triumphs or Festivals.   (XI. 722-23)

In the Cambridge Manuscript occur two titles on this subject, "The flood," and "The Deluge." There is nothing more. This, however, does not prove that Milton was but slightly interested. The Cambridge Manuscript is not a complete collection of Milton's notes, but an assembly of pages once scattered. In what we have, the mere subject "Moabitides Num. 25" occurs on one sheet; yet on another, where there happened to be room, is an outline of some seventy-five words for a tragedy of the same name.[1] A draft for a drama on the Flood may have been written on a page now lacking. It is not incredible that Milton wrote such a play.[2] One of its main features would be a vigor-

---

1. See Fig. 3.
2. I am accepting the usual and probable assumption that all the Biblical subjects are for dramas. Most of them evidently are, but one should at least recall the words of J. Holly Hanford: The Scriptural subjects "are not, like the British themes, specifically designated as tragedies, and some, for example 'Samaria liberata,' suggest the epic form."—"The Dramatic Element in *Paradise*

Lost," *Studies in Philology*, XIV (1917), 192.

It supports Hanford's suggestion that even among the "British Trag." there is a reference to a heroic poem on King Alfred. One should note, however, that between Plans One and Two for the tragedy of *Paradise Lost* Milton wrote "other Tragedies" and listed *Adam in Banishment*, *The flood*, and *Abram in AEgypt*. The title *Samaria liberata* suggests

ous description by some witness, an angel perhaps. Obviously such a speaker would depend on, but much enlarge, the Biblical account. Is the description in xi. 712-53 derived from such a tragedy?

Yet there is little basis for assuming that either account of Noah and the Deluge is the older or the later. The second and simpler one, since it is narrated by the angel in the future tense, may come from a time when Milton had not yet decided on the device of visions for informing Adam of the future but was allowing the angel merely to narrate what is to come. But the revision for fitting each of the two into its place has been such that there can be no certainty. Probably there remain indications of two diverse plans not consolidated. At least Milton failed either to remove repetition or to give unmistakable signs of its function.

5. Changes in Climate
(x. 651-95, 1062-66)

AFTER THE Judgment of man, the Almighty "commands his Angels to make several alterations in the Heavens and Elements" (x. Arg.) in order to convert the equable climate of Paradise to one suited to a sinful world. The Angels at once undertake their task. Then

> These changes in the Heav'ns, though slow, produc'd
> Like change on Sea and Land, sideral blast,
> Vapour, and Mist, and Exhalation hot,
> Corrupt and Pestilent,   (x. 692-95)

and there follows a list of all the fierce winds that disturb the hitherto-balmy Garden. The changes are said to be "slow," yet Adam "alreadie" sees all his growing miseries (x. 715); the night is

> with black Air
> Accompanied, with damps and dreadful gloom,   (x. 847-48)

the ground is cold, and the next day he speaks of learning

> to shun
> Th' inclement Seasons, Rain, Ice, Hail and Snow,

Tasso's epic, yet the subject is perhaps better suited for tragedy than is the Flood, which Milton gives as a dramatic subject.

> Which now the Skie with various Face begins
> To shew us in this Mountain, while the Winds
> Blow moist and keen.   (x. 1062-66)

Eternal spring is a thing of the past. Before Michael reaches the Garden on his errand of expulsion, the air is "suddenly eclips'd After short blush of Morn" and there is "darkness ere Dayes mid-course" (xi. 183-84, 204). The whole narrative gives the effect of changes not "slow" but, like the eclipsing of the air, sudden. Why did Milton insert the qualification *though slow?*

The astronomical passage containing the words is somewhat strangely handled; it begins in the midst of a paragraph of which the first part gives a few lines of angelic song on God's justice and on Messiah as restorer. The Sun is more than once alluded to.

> The Sun
> Had first his precept so to move, so shine,
> As might affect the Earth with cold and heat
> Scarce tollerable.   (x. 651-54)

Then, as an alternative,

> Som say the Sun
> Was bid turn Reines from th'Equinoctial Rode
> . . . . to bring in change
> Of Seasons to each Clime.   (x. 671-78)

Further,

> At that tasted Fruit
> The Sun, as from *Thyestean* Banquet, turn'd
> His course intended; else how had the World
> Inhabited, though sinless, more then now,
> Avoided pinching cold and scorching heate?   (x. 687-91)

In the last, the personified Sun acts according to his own feelings rather than, as in the other two, receiving divine orders. The first two are not in agreement, for in one the change in the Sun accomplishes everything, in the other there is astronomical debate. Following each of the three the changes in earthly climate are given, with some verbal repetition. Still further, after we are told what the winds "now" do, come the lines:

> Thus began
> Outrage from liveless things; but Discord first
> Daughter of Sin, among th'irrational,
> Death introduc'd through fierce antipathie.   (x. 706-9)

The word *first* apparently means *before that,* so that the work of Discord comes before the changes in climate. Is it possible that the context was once so arranged that antipathy among the animals did come first and slow changes in climate followed?[1] Were even some of these verses planned for the drama of *Adam in Banishment,* listed in the Cambridge Manuscript? That work certainly would have made much reference to Adam's sufferings from cold and heat, wet and dry. At least, some of these passages seem not to have been composed under the present plan.

6. The Nature of the Garden of Eden
(IV. 133-42, 174-77, 543-48)

WHEN SATAN draws near the Garden for the first time, he sees that Paradise

> Crowns with her enclosure green,
> As with a rural mound the champain head
> Of a steep wilderness, whose hairie sides
> With thicket overgrown, grottesque and wilde,
> Access deni'd; and over head up grew
> Insuperable highth of loftiest shade,
> Cedar, and Pine, and Firr, and branching Palm,

1. As the poem now stands Milton deals with sudden change rather than with a gradual one such as he mentions in *Naturam non pati senium:*

> Num tetra vetustas
> Annorumque aeterna fames,
>   squalorque situsque
> Sidera vexabunt?   (12-14)

The change Adam sees is not of the type mentioned in Spenser's *Mutability;* it is rather from a benign state to one in which the works of Mutability appear:

> Now boyling hot; streight friezing deadly cold;
> Now faire sun-shine, that makes all skip and daunce;
> Streight bitter storms, and balefull countenaunce
> That makes them all to shiver and to shake:
> Rayne, hayle, and snowe do pay them sad penance,
> And dreadfull thunder-claps (that make them quake)
> With flames and flashing lights that thousand changes make.
>   (VII. 23)

> A Silvan Scene, and as the ranks ascend
> Shade above shade, a woodie Theatre
> Of stateliest view.   (IV. 133-42)

Seeking to ascend "that steep savage Hill,"[1] he finds no way,

> so thick entwin'd,
> As one continu'd brake, the undergrowth
> Of shrubs and tangling bushes had perplext
> All path of Man or Beast that past that way.   (IV. 174-77)

Likewise when Adam is first taken into the Garden he is led "up A woodie Mountain" (VIII. 302). Yet when Paradise is described by means of comparisons, we read of Mount Amara

> under the Ethiop Line
> By Nilus head, enclosd with shining Rock.   (IV. 282-83)

When again alluded to, the mountain is like Amara:

> It was a Rock
> Of Alablaster, pil'd up to the Clouds,
> Conspicuous farr, winding with one ascent
> Accessible from Earth, one entrance high;
> The rest was craggie cliff, that overhung
> Still as it rose, impossible to climbe.[2]   (IV. 543-48)

Later the angel lights "on th' Eastern cliff of Paradise" (v. 275), and when our parents are expelled they are led "down the Cliff" (XII. 639). In other words, Milton changes from a thickly wooded hill with sides steep but possible of ascent, except for the bushes and trees, to a mount with overhanging cliffs.[3] So long as Eden is a "shaggie Hill" (IV. 224), there is no hint of angelic guardians,[4] but when the craggie, overhanging cliff of Mt. Amara is adopted, they are present (IV. 549). When Raphael comes he passes them (v. 287). According to Purchas,

1. Cf. "shaggie Hill" (IV. 224).
2. Allan H. Gilbert, *A Geographical Dictionary of Milton* (New Haven, 1919), *s.v.*, Amara.
3. This and other discrepancies are noted in the study of the "disjunctive composition" of *Paradise Lost* by Professor Grant McColley, in his *Paradise Lost*, Chapters 11 and 12. I hope I have allowed nothing in these chapters to escape me; this acknowledgement is intended to stand for several.

4. The "senteries" of Beelzebub's speech (II. 412) possibly include the guards in Paradise.

such watchmen protected Amara;[5] hence the cliffs are easily associated with the guardianship of the angels. Probably the two conceptions indicate different times of composition. Mt. Amara, being associated with the angelic guards, who play in Draft Four much the same part as in *Paradise Lost*, is perhaps the earlier; indeed the description of Paradise by Gabriel according to Plan Four might have involved hints from Mt. Amara.[6] Could the lines (IV. 268-83) where the Garden of Eden is compared with various lovely spots actually have been written for the drama? The passages in which the hill is shaggy are associated with activities by Satan which are not suggested in Plan Four and perhaps were added when the work was written as an epic. Adam's creation, in connection with which the mountain is "woodie" (VIII. 302), is also not mentioned in Plan Four, though that of Eve is. It seems not unlikely then, that the Mount of Paradise was first like Mt. Amara and that the notion of a wooded mountain came later.

7. Satan Captured in the Garden
(IV. 797-1015)

AFTER SATAN enters the universe he speeds to the Sun, where he deceives the sharp-sighted Uriel (III. 681 ff.). Descending to Mt. Niphates, Satan allows his true feelings to appear and is marked by "Uriel once warnd" (IV. 125). The meaning of "once warnd" is not clear. No aid is furnished by the plans for tragedies, in which Satan seems to come unexpectedly upon the guardians; Uriel in the Sun is an epic concept. From *warnd* one postulates a suggestion given to Uriel after the conversation in the Sun, as he then gives it to Gabriel. But there would then be two forewarnings—something not very likely. There is even lack of agreement in other ways. Satan is sad and speaks with sighs (IV. 31) and the tone of his speech is melancholy; he is "disfigur'd," but only "more then could befall Spirit of happie sort" (IV. 127-28). This is not quite in harmony with "his gestures fierce" and especially his "mad demeanour," for, though he was "inflam'd with

---

5. The "Ivorie Port" of IV. 778 has not been satisfactorily explained; it suggests a building intended for the guard, more suitable for Purchas' Amara

than for Paradise.

6. See Milton's Plan for a Tragedy, Prologue, in Sec. 2, above, and Fig. 2.

rage" and his attempt was boiling in his breast, he still seems to have kept his hell "within him" (IV. 9-20). Meditative melancholy and furious wrath are not consistent with each other.

At any rate, Uriel descends to the Garden of Eden and warns Gabriel that "one of the banisht crew" (IV. 573) has ventured there. Gabriel sends out Ithuriel and Zephon, who find Satan at the ear of Eve and bring him to their commander. Sarcastic and insulting speeches on both sides lead toward combat, but Satan, seeing his lot weighed in the heavenly scales and found light, flees (IV. 1015). He does not again appear until, as the crisis approaches,

> Satan who late fled before the threats
> Of Gabriel out of Eden, now improv'd
> In meditated fraud and malice, bent
> On mans destruction, maugre what might hap
> Of heavier on himself, fearless return'd.   (IX. 53-7)

In order to avoid Uriel and the "cherubic watch," he returns at midnight and does not use the eastern entrance-gate. He is able to carry through the Temptation without interference, for the guardians know nothing of it until after the Fall, when they hasten to Heaven to assert their vigilance (x. 30). They are not censured, for the Almighty announces:

> Assembl'd Angels, and ye Powers return'd
> From unsuccessful charge, be not dismaid,
> Nor troubl'd at these tidings from the Earth,
> Which your sincerest care could not prevent,
> Foretold so lately what would come to pass,
> When first this Tempter cross'd the Gulf from Hell.
> I told ye then he should prevail and speed
> On his bad Errand.   (x. 34-41)

So far as the main course of the action is concerned, the guardians of Paradise might as well not have been put there; even their arrest of Satan can have no result more important than a delay in the execution of his plan; nothing so elaborate is needed to give opportunity for Raphael's warning to Adam. The futility of their watch is accented by their release of the Adversary even though he is not strong enough to resist them (IV. 1012-14). It had to be so, because the Biblical story required that Satan be free to succeed.

Since Uriel is associated with the attempt by Satan in none of the dramatic plans but only in the finished poem, and his position in the Sun is an epic conception, we can suppose that his part was devised when Milton was working on the heroic form. But it must have been early in the composition of that form,[1] early enough at least to permit of subsequent revision in the course of which the scene of warning disappeared, leaving behind some puzzling vestiges.

In the fourth plan for a drama the episode of Satan and the watch occurs in the same resultless form as in the epic: "Lucifer . . . seeks revenge on man the Chorus prepare resistance at his first approach at last after discourse of enmity on either side he departs whereat the chorus sings of the battell, & victorie in heavn against him."[2] Evidently part of the epic story is developed from this, though with the additions of the discovery of Satan by the two angels, an action not hinted at in Draft Four.

Parts of the story of the arrest are now inconsistent. Gabriel tells Ithuriel and Zephon of the coming of "som infernal Spirit" who has escaped from Hell and orders them to arrest him:

> Such where ye find, seise fast, and hither bring.   (IV. 796)

The angels do not execute this order literally; they ask him to come (IV. 841) and he obeys,

> But like a proud Steed reind, went hautie on,
> Chaumping his iron curb: to strive or flie

1. Yet revision at least was apparently later than the late change of the victors in the War in Heaven from the angels to the Son (Secs. 35; 50, Group VI) if weight can be given to Satan's words:

Insulting Angel, well thou knowst I stood
Thy fiercest, when in Battel to thy aide
The blasting volied Thunder made all speed

And seconded thy else not dreaded Spear.
                                (IV. 926-29)

This seems to refer to the coming of the Son armed with the Father's thunder on the last day of the War in Heaven (VI. 764, 836; note especially line 854: "mid Volie").

2. See Milton's Plans for a Tragedy, Act II, in Sec. 2, above, and Fig. 2.

> He held it vain; awe from above had quelld
> His heart, not else dismai'd. (IV. 858-61)

Yet when Satan is brought before Gabriel, he no longer holds resistance vain but collects his might for a conflict in which perhaps "all the Elements At least had gone to rack." Evidently he is released from "awe from above," though only for the moment, for again, on seeing "his mounted scale aloft," he flees from the vain combat. Why did Milton thus rapidly alternate the Adversary's state of mind?

At least the poet has taken various precautions to make his procedure plausible. When the two angels find Satan, he excuses his meekness in submitting to arrest, boasting that he will contest with

> the Sender not the sent,
> Or all at once, (IV. 852-3)

and when the three draw near the squadron, Gabriel remarks that the Prince of Hell is

> Not likely to part hence without contest. (IV. 872)

But such remarks only gloss over the unlikelihood that under any provocation one man who submits to arrest by two should then prepare to fight a squadron led by such a warrior as Gabriel. It appears that in the tragedy Satan would have encountered the angelic guards in numbers no larger than would form a chorus and not under the leadership of Gabriel. Conflict between Satan and them would be more probable than at present. When Milton added Satan's attempt on Eve and the arrest by the two angels, he still did not wish to abandon his earlier plan for threat of conflict.

In the drama the unbiblical watchmen did not come on the stage, as they enter the epic, merely to catch Satan or to act more generally as guardians of Paradise. They are the chorus indispensable to such a play, whose presence is made likely by giving them duty as guards. In this function they naturally encounter Satan, though without keeping him permanently from the garden. In the poem, since no chorus was needed, Milton could·have dispensed with his guards and their fruitless watch.[3] But he had grown accustomed to them as part of his

---

3. Dr. Johnson writes: "Satan is with great expectation brought before Gabriel in Paradise, and is suffered to go away unmolested" ("Milton", par. 259, in *English Poets* [Oxford, 1905], I, 186).

plan and liked the scene of their meeting with the Prince of Darkness. So from the drama the chorus, deprived of its original function, came over into the epic, where it supplies a means for emphasizing Satan's weakness, which in the tragedy appeared in the succeeding song on his defeat in Heaven. In the epic the encounter with the angelic guards serves to remind the reader that, as Gabriel says:

> I know thy strength, and thou knowst mine,
> Neither our own but giv'n; what follie then
> To boast what Arms can doe, since thine no more
> Then Heav'n permits, nor mine.   (IV. 1006-9)

It makes concrete what we are often told in the poem, that God could have protected man, but preferred rather to leave him his independence and free will to choose good or evil as he would. An unrestrained Devil is the symbol of man's liberty. The passage adds, too, an element of which Sir Walter Raleigh wrote:

Even in *Paradise Lost,* his education in the handling of satire and invective stood him in stead. The poem contains more than one "flyting"—to use the Scottish term—and the high war of words between . . . Satan and Gabriel on earth, could not have been handled save by a master of all the weapons of verbal fence and all the devices of wounding invective. In the great close of the fourth book, especially, where the arch-fiend and the archangel retaliate defiance, and tower, in swift alternate flights, to higher and higher pitches of exultant scorn, Milton puts forth all his strength, and brings into action a whole armoury of sarcasm and insult whetted and polished from its earlier prosaic exercise.[4]

8. The Genial Angel
(IV. 467-76, 710-14; VIII. 484-87)

IN HER first speech, Eve, after telling of her Narcissus-like experience, continues:

> A voice thus warnd me . . .
> . . . . follow me,
> And I will bring thee where no shadow staies

4. *Milton* (London, 1900), pp. 72-73.

> Thy coming, and thy soft imbraces, hee
> Whose image thou art, him thou shalt enjoy
> Inseparablie thine, to him shalt beare
> Multitudes like thy self, and thence be call'd
> Mother of human Race: what could I doe,
> But follow strait, invisibly thus led?   (IV. 467-76)

This agrees with Adam's account to Raphael:

> On she came,
> Led by her Heav'nly Maker, though unseen,
> And guided by his voice, nor uninformd
> Of nuptial Sanctitie and marriage Rites.   (VIII. 484-87)

Yet the poet himself represents her as brought not by her Maker but by the angel of marriage:

> Espoused Eve deckt first her nuptial Bed,
> And heav'nly Quires the Hymenaean sung,
> What day the genial Angel to our Sire
> Brought her in naked beauty more adorn'd,
> More lovely then Pandora.   (IV. 710-14)

All three passages have some relation to the plans in the Cambridge Manuscript. In Plan Four the angel Gabriel tells of "the creation of Eve with thire love, & mariage." In Draft Three an entire act is given to the marriage, with the aid of Heavenly Love and Evening Star, and "the Chorus sing the mariage song." Possible reminiscences occur often in Book IV, as in lines 598-609, 641-56, 690-715, 737-73.[1]

It may be noted that the first and third passages quoted are from the same book, some 240 lines apart. If this book was composed as a unit, such a divergence would be unlikely; if there has been much revision, some sign of an early plan may well occur. Presumably the presence of the Maker himself, otherwise so prominent in Adam's report in the eighth book, marks the later form. The concept of an invisible guide is well suited to narrative verse. The second act of Draft Three is entirely devoted to the marriage; it must have contemplated much activity by the personified Heavenly Love and Evening Star and by the chorus of angels. Doubtless a "genial angel,"

1. Note also the Evening Star in VIII. 519.

a sort of Hymen adapted to a Biblical setting, played a part, now indicated only by a single reference that has survived his replacement
by the Maker himself.

9. The Poet in His Own Person
(III. 412-15; V. 202-4)

THE MORNING hymn of Adam and Eve uses the words *us* (v. 157,
206) and *our* (v. 184), thus indicating that it is intended for both
Adam and Eve. But toward the end are the lines:

> Witness if I be silent, Morn or Eeven,
> To Hill, or Valley, Fountain, or fresh shade
> Made vocal by my Song.   (v. 202-4)

One of the instances of *us* immediately follows. Who is *I?*

There are (besides those in the introductions to Books I, III, VII,
and IX) a few other instances of the first person not apparently applying to a character in the poem. After the Son offers himself as redeemer,
the angels sing his praises. At the end, in the same paragraph, appear
the lines:

> Hail Son of God, Saviour of Men, thy Name
> Shall be the copious matter of my Song
> Henceforth, and never shall my Harp thy praise
> Forget, nor from thy Fathers praise disjoine.   (III. 412-15)

The song is introduced with the words: "Thee Father first they sung"
(III. 372). The effect is that *I* means John Milton, speaking at the end
of a lyric. The hymn is so related to the subject of *Paradise Lost* that
on first sight it seems well integrated; note especially the references
to the overthrow of Satan by the Son riding in a chariot (III. 394).
The construction is, however, peculiar. The song begins by telling
what the angels sang about the Father and then turns to direct address.
The same method is used for the part on the Son (III. 383-400). Then
there is direct address to the "Father of Mercie and Grace," whose
wrath is appeased by the Son. A slight change would render the structure normal; the poem might begin: "Thee Father first I sing"; and so
might be treated the address to the Son. We then should have a lyric
in which the speaker is not Milton himself, but perhaps an angelic

singer in the drama of *Paradise Lost*. Otherwise the lines in the first person must be thought an independent utterance by the poet, though they continue the hymn directly.

Instances of *I* in Book IV, lines 741, 758, obviously refer to John Milton.

In VI. 373, *I* occurs as though in the mouth of Raphael, but seems rather to mean again the author, who failed to eliminate a pronoun fitting when the war in Heaven was narrated by himself rather than by one of his characters.[1]

The analogies suggest that the morning hymn of our first parents was once a lyric for a single speaker and that the plural pronouns refer to mankind. Such a theory may be taken to imply that Milton wrote lyrics, probably for his dramas, in blank verse. If so, this change from the practice of *Comus* and *Samson Agonistes* would indicate that when composing dramatic lyrics Milton acted on the objections to rime he expressed in "The Verse" prefixed to *Paradise Lost*. It is more probable that such a lyric was originally in rimed verse and was rewritten in its present form.

10. Adam's Presumption
(x. 48-53, 210-11, 771-811, 1046-50; XI. 195-99, 252-55)

IN THE COURSE of instructing the Son on the judgment of man, the Almighty says:

> What rests but that the mortal Sentence pass
> On his transgression, Death denounc't that day,
> Which he presumes already vain and void,
> Because not yet inflicted, as he fear'd,
> By some immediate stroak; but soon shall find
> Forbearance no aquittance ere day end.   (x. 48-53)

The tone of the passage, and especially the word *presumes*, indicate a charge against man of presumption or overboldness, yet man has not asserted that the sentence is vain. Eve says that the "Serpent wise" on taking of the fruit

1. This is explained as "referring to the poet himself" by Laura E. Lockwood, *Lexicon to Milton* (New York, 1907). See Sec. 14, below.

> is become,
> Not dead, as we are threaten'd,   (IX. 869-70)

and Adam thinks that perhaps, since the Serpent has profaned the fruit,
Eve will not die, or even that God is not in earnest (IX. 939), but yet
he admits that in tasting he runs the risk of death. Eve, when disclaim-
ing any thought of bringing death on her husband, concludes:

> On my experience, *Adam*, freely taste,
> And fear of Death deliver to the Windes.   (IX. 988-89)

There are some later references to the immediacy of punishment
after taking the fruit. The Son in his judgment of fallen man

> th'instant stroke of Death denounc't that day
> Remov'd farr off.   (X. 210-11)

Adam possibly has caught something of this; at least he reasons on the
matter:

> Why delayes
> His hand to execute what his Decree
> Fixd on this day? why do I overlive,
> Why am I mockt with death, and length'nd out
> To deathless pain . . . .
> . . . . But say
> That Death be not one stroak, as I suppos'd,
> Bereaving sense, but endless miserie
> From this day onward.   (X. 771-811)

He recurs more evidently to the Judgment:

> Remember with what mild
> And gracious temper he both heard and judg'd
> Without wrauth or reviling; wee expected
> Immediate dissolution, which we thought
> Was meant by Death that day.   (X. 1046-50)

Still he is uncertain; seeing violence among the animals in the Garden,
he wonders with Eve whether it is

> to warn
> Us haply too secure of our discharge
> From penaltie, because from death releast

>Some days; how long, and what till then our life,
>Who knows.   (XI. 195-99)

This is a reminder of the Almighty's words on Adam's presuming. Michael before the expulsion from the Garden confirms the postponement of the last penalty:

>Death,
>Then due by sentence when thou didst transgress,
>[Is] Defeated of his seisure many dayes
>Giv'n thee of Grace.   (XI. 252-55)

Adam does not, then, express any certainty that the "immediate stroak" of death will be postponed, though if he had done so he would have been right. Nor does he or Eve think the denunciation of the penalty "vain and void" because postponed. Eve does think it void for other reasons, and Adam, with doubt, echoes her words. If Adam's presumption, as set forth by the Almighty, is to be connected with other parts of the poem, it is not consistent. We may then suppose that in one stage of his work Milton had Adam utter the sentiments attributed to him by God. The tragedy according to Draft Four would have given a place for such conduct; at least Adam is "stubborn in his offence" and is warned against impenitence.[1] Though deciding, as he worked further, to omit Adam's bold assumption, Milton failed to delete the Almighty's charge against him.

11. Satan in the Serpent
(X. 169-74, 1030-35)

THOUGH ADAM was warned against Satan by Raphael and though he knew that the tempter would use such guile (IX. 306) that his reason and that of Eve might

>   meet
>Some specious object by the Foe subornd,
>And fall into deception unaware,   (IX. 360-62)

he did not realize that the snake was not a mere animal. He rebukes his wife:

1. See Milton's Plan for a Tragedy, Act IV, in Sec. 2, above, and Fig. 2.

> O *Eve*, in evil hour thou didst give eare
> To that false Worm, of whomsoever taught
> To counterfeit Mans voice;   (IX. 1067-69)

he even tells her that she thought she could overcome Satan himself but was fooled and beguiled by the mere serpent (x. 880). She too accuses "that cruel Serpent," not extending her blame to the Devil (x. 927). In harmony with their ignorance, the poet comments on the Lord God's judgment:

> More to know
> Concern'd not Man (since he no further knew)
> Nor alter'd his offence; yet God at last
> To Satan first in sin his doom apply'd,
> Though in mysterious terms, judg'd as then best:
> And on the Serpent thus his curse let fall.[1]   (x. 169-74)

Adam, however, soon tells Eve that he has penetrated the mystery,

> calling to minde with heed
> Part of our Sentence, that thy Seed shall bruise
> The Serpents head; piteous amends, unless
> Be meant, whom I conjecture, our grand Foe
> *Satan*, who in the Serpent hath contriv'd
> Against us this deceit.   (x. 1030-35)

So far as the poem is concerned, this conjecture is all the information

1. It may seem that there is an inconsistency between two references to the treatment of the Serpent. The Son says:

> The third best absent is condemn'd,
> Convict by flight, and Rebel to all Law
> Conviction to the Serpent none belongs.   (x. 82-84)

Yet when the Lord God heard Eve accuse the Serpent,

> without delay
> To Judgement he proceeded on th' accus'd

Serpent though brute.
(x. 163-65)

The word *conviction* signifies *proof of guilt*, a legal trial as it were, such as is given Adam and Eve, who have an opportunity to defend themselves, while the Serpent does not. Hence the words *without delay* in the second quotation take up the *absent* of the first one; the Judge did not need to spend time in asking for the Serpent. The judgment of the Serpent is so clear in Genesis 3:14-15 that Milton can hardly have written anything indicating that it did not occur.

Adam ever has. When Michael descends for the expulsion God instructs him to

> Intermix
> My Cov'nant in the womans seed renewd.   (xi. 115-16)

Meanwhile Adam has already, after prayer, become certain that, as he says to Eve, "thy Seed shall bruise our Foe" (xi. 155); it may be noted that though the "foe" is not named as Lucifer, the Serpent is not mentioned. When Michael reveals the seed of the woman as the Son of God, Adam is still not wholly clear, exclaiming

> Needs must the Serpent now his capital bruise
> Expect with mortal paine: say where and when
> Thir fight, what stroke shall bruise the Victors heel.
>
> (xii. 383-85)

Even then Michael, neglecting the mere reptile, assumes Adam's knowledge that the tempter was

> *Satan*, whose fall from Heav'n, a deadlier bruise,
> Disabl'd not to give thee thy deaths wound,   (xii. 391-92)

and further speaks of bruising the head of Satan (line 430), and of "the Serpent, Prince of aire" (line 454), without explaining. Adam, however, understands that he means

> The Womans seed, obscurely then foretold,
> Now amplier known thy Saviour and thy Lord,
> Last in the Clouds from Heav'n to be reveald
> In glory of the Father, to dissolve
> *Satan* with his perverted World.   (xii. 543-47)

It would not cause any surprise that no explanation is given of how Adam came to know something so common in theology,[2] if it were not that he is represented as ignorant, especially at the Judgment. Would Milton have so dwelt on lack of knowledge if it were not to be specifically remedied? He must have intended that in some way, as through Michael, Adam would learn the truth. Yet it is not necessary to suppose that he ever actually wrote out any such plain information. The greater piece of information, namely that the seed of

2. Cf. the Argument of Book I.

the woman is the Son of God, naturally carries with it the lesser one of the Devil's disguise. Having attended to the important thing, Milton may not have observed that he had not dealt with the subsidiary one. It is not unlikely that the explanation of the mysterious verdict was planned as part of the promise of the Messiah by Mercy at the end of the tragedy of Draft Four.[3] This disappeared in the transformation to the later tragedy and to the epic, and at the same time there came into the epic the assumption that Adam knew of the power within the Serpent.

12. The Two Satans
(I. 195-209; IV. 400-2, 985-95; IX. 482-88; X. 332-44, 528-32)

In MILTON's third draft for the tragedy of *Paradise Lost*, Lucifer appears in but one act, "contriving Adams ruine." The scene of the Fall is unmentioned. The fourth draft has Lucifer appear also after the Fall, "relating, & insulting in what he had don to the destruction of man." In the fifth plan he appeared in soliloquy at the beginning, though perhaps Milton still refrained from presenting on the stage the temptation of Eve by the serpent.[1] Satan's importance seems to have grown as Milton planned further, so that the Fifth Plan may have shown—or perhaps only narrated—much of Satan's activity in the Garden.

But when the epic stage was reached, the Satan of the War in Heaven and of the scenes in Hell had to be devised. When first seen on the burning lake, he,

>   extended long and large
> Lay floating many a rood, in bulk as huge
> As whom the Fables name of monstrous size,
> *Titanian*, or *Earth-born*, that warr'd on *Jove*,
> *Briareos* or *Typhon*, whom the Den
> By ancient *Tarsus* held, or that Sea-beast
> *Leviathan*, which God of all his works
> Created hugest that swim th'Ocean stream:
>
> . . . .
>
> So stretcht out huge in length the Arch-fiend lay. (I. 195-209)

3. See Milton's Plans for a Tragedy,   1. See Sec. 2, above.
   Act V, in Sec. 2, above, and
   Fig. 2.

If Milton planned his tragedy with the slightest relation to the stage, such a huge Satan is impossible. All characters, as in Andreini's *Adamo*, must be of normal human size, and—partly that nothing is said of the size of angel-visitors—so it appears they are. The only exception is when, about to fight with Gabriel and the guardians of Paradise,

> Satan allarm'd
> Collecting all his might dilated stood,
> Like *Teneriff* or *Atlas* unremov'd:
> His stature reacht the Skie, and on his Crest
> Sat horror Plum'd; . . . . .
> . . . . . . now dreadful deeds
> Might have ensu'd, nor onely Paradise
> In this commotion, but the Starrie Cope
> Of Heav'n perhaps, or all the Elements
> At least had gon to rack, disturbd and torne
> With violence of this conflict.[2]   (iv. 985-95)

This is the Satan of the celestial conflict, in which, as the angels hurl "main Promontories," all Heaven would have "gone to wrack, with ruin overspred" (vi. 670), had not the Almighty interfered. Though the idea of combat between Satan and the guardian angels of Paradise goes back to the fourth draft, it seems likely that the passage just quoted on Satan's huge size is later than references to it in Books I and VI.

Moreover, when Satan, rather than directing a host of giants such that

> never since created man,
> Met such imbodied force, as nam'd with these
> Could merit more then that small infantry
> Warr'd on by Cranes,   (i. 573-6)

is playing a lone hand in the Garden, he proceeds by craft rather than might. On his way to the Earth he tricks Uriel through a dis-

---

2. It may be recalled that Ariosto, when he sets out to be extravagant, makes the encounter of two of his human knights approach such an effect on nature:

Fe' lo scontro tremar dal basso all'alto
L'erbose valli insino ai poggi ignudi.
    (*Orlando Furioso*, 1.62)
Cf. 7.6; 19.92; 24.100; 41.69, 73.

guise. Coming on Adam and Eve when they think themselves alone
(IV. 340), he enters into various animals

> Neerer to view his prey, and unespi'd
> To mark what of thir state he more might learn
> By word or action markt.   (IV. 400-2)

From this eavesdropping he learns of the Tree of Knowledge. But
wishing to know more, he plans to trick "some wandring Spirit of
Heaven," for whom he searches "with sly circumspection."[3] Next
he is found, "squat like a toad," at the ear of Eve, tempting her in a
dream. He is surprised by Ithuriel and Zephon, to whom he submits.[4]
Then comes his defiance of Gabriel. Yet even here he does not come
to violence but, on seeing "His mounted scale aloft, . . . fled Mur-
muring" (IV. 1014-15). Nothing of his defiance of Gabriel appears
in his next action, even though he "fearless return'd" (IX. 57), for he

> on the Coast averse
> From entrance or Cherubic Watch, by stealth
> Found unsuspected way.   (IX. 67-69)

Having debased himself to the serpent, he congratulates himself on
meeting Eve alone,

> Her Husband, for I view far round, not nigh,
> Whose higher intellectual more I shun,
> And strength, of courage hautie, and of limb
> Heroic built, though of terrestrial mould,
> Foe not informidable, exempt from wound,
> I not; so much hath Hell debas'd, and paine
> Infeebl'd me, to what I was in Heav'n.   (IX. 482-88)

Still less heroic is his conduct after he has accomplished his fraud
on Eve:

> Hee after *Eve* seduc't, unminded slunk
> Into the Wood fast by, and changing shape
> To observe the sequel, saw his guileful act
> By *Eve*, though all unweeting, seconded
> Upon her Husband, saw thir shame that sought
> Vain covertures; but when he saw descend

3. IV. 531, 537. See Sec. 26, below.   4. See Sec. 7, above.

> The Son of God to judge them terrifi'd
> Hee fled, not hoping to escape, but shun
> The present, fearing guiltie what his wrauth
> Might suddenly inflict; that past, return'd
> By Night, and listening where the hapless Paire
> Sate in thir sad discourse, and various plaint,
> Thence gatherd his own doom.   (x. 332-44)

He is still the eavesdropper, now crouching in darkness.

But at once he returns to Hell and resumes his dauntlessness as well as his huge size; at least he is "A monstrous Serpent,"

> greatest hee the midst,
> Now Dragon grown, larger then whom the Sun
> Ingenderd in the *Pythian* Vale on slime,
> Huge *Python*, and his Power no less he seem'd
> Above the rest still to retain.   (x. 528-32)

This passage is presumably later than even those in the first two books with which it harmonizes.[5]

It is evident that though the Lucifer of the tragedy and the Satan of the epic have in common many traits, such as unshaking perseverance in envy and revenge, they are yet as distinct as their different settings indicate. The words of many writers on his character refer primarily to the epic rather than the dramatic Satan.[6] For example Coleridge wrote:

The character of Satan is pride and sensual indulgence, finding in self the sole motive of action. It is the character so often seen *in little* on the political stage. It exhibits all the restlessness, temerity, and cunning which have marked the mighty hunters of mankind from

5. See Sec. 39, below.

6. For the most recent phase of the controversy over Satan's character, see C. S. Lewis, *A Preface to Paradise Lost* (London, 1942), pp. 92-100; Elmer Edgar Stoll, "Give the Devil His Due: A Reply to Mr. Lewis," *Review of English Studies*, XX (1944), 108-24; G. Rostrevor Hamilton, *Hero or Fool? A Study of Milton's Satan* (London, 1944); Allan H. Gilbert, "The Controversy over Milton's Satan," to appear in *The South Atlantic Quarterly*.

The well-known but, as I think, untenable idea of Satan's progressive degeneration (except as strictly confined to such passages as VI. 691-92) is probably in part a result of perceiving that Satan is not to be assigned to a single type.

Nimrod to Napoleon. The common fascination of men is, that these great men, as they are called, must act from some great motive. Milton has carefully marked in his Satan the intense selfishness, the alcohol of egotism, which would rather reign in hell than serve in heaven. To place this lust of self in opposition to denial of self or duty, and to show what exertions it would make, and what pains endure to accomplish its end, is Milton's particular object in the character of Satan. But around this character he has thrown a singularity of daring, a grandeur of sufferance, and a ruined splendour, which constitute the very height of poetic sublimity (Remains of Lecture X, 1818).

While parts of this, such as the word *cunning*, evidently can apply to Satan in the Garden, as a whole it is marked by the references to Napoleon and to reigning in Hell as derived chiefly from Books I, II, V, and VI. The three phrases of praise in the last sentence in particular apply chiefly to the Devil of those books, rather than to the Satan of Book IX, who is "cautious" (ix. 59), though still fearlessly bent on man's destruction.

It is easy to say that the critics should have attended more than they have to the less spectacular parts of Lucifer's career. Yet Milton is himself in part responsible. The Satan of the garden—except when with Gabriel—is hardly fitted to take the part of the opponent in an epic action, but must be magnified until he can play Hector to Michael as Achilles, or Rodomonte to the angel's Ruggiero. Moreover, Milton wished the forces of evil to appear tremendous, as befits their importance in the present world. Satan is indeed utterly helpless against the Calvinistic God; thrust into Hell by divine power,

> the Arch-fiend lay
> Chain'd on the burning Lake, nor ever thence
> Had ris'n or heav'd his head, but that the will
> And high permission of all-ruling Heaven
> Left him at large to his own dark designs.   (i. 209-13)

But when the Almighty unchains the giant, the power let loose is such as worthily to express the might of free will with which man can resist the Adversary. So far as this Satan, standing for the universal power of evil, is not to be reconciled with the villain of the garden-tragedy, a critic cannot arrive at a unified characterization of the Adversary.

Milton brought the two conceptions—never wholly diverse—into such agreement as his purpose required, but not further; indeed it seems that his intention demanded two harmonized concepts of Satan rather than one only. The guileful tempter of the Garden is derived chiefly from Milton's labors on his tragedy and the "Superior Fiend" as sultan over a host of giants is an epic conception.

CHAPTER FOUR

THE MIDDLE EPIC SHIFT OF THE WAR IN HEAVEN

THE preceding part has dealt with real or seeming inconsistencies in *Paradise Lost* as a result of the taking over into the epic of matter wholly or partly brought into form for one of Milton's tragedies. The present part (Sections 13-18) is concerned with the most striking hypothesis considered in this volume, namely that the narrative of the War in Heaven, now related by Raphael, was once not in the midst, but at the very beginning of the epic, then in chronological order. The following part (sections 19-25) deals with a similar notion, that is, that Book VII, the account of the Creation expanded from Genesis, was also not originally given to Raphael or in its present position, but that it too came earlier in the epic and as nearly as possible in the order of time. Section 25 includes a table of the hypothetical arrangement of the poem before these two portions were put in their present places.

13. In Medias Res

(1. Argument)

THE NOTION that *Paradise Lost* was first arranged in chronological order may be objected to on the ground that the epic presumes beginning the action in the midst, rather than at the beginning, and supplying the early part by the narrative of a character, such as Raphael or Aeneas. In discussing the matter, *Paradise Lost* itself must first be eliminated. It is the most evident exemplar of the method of narrating what takes place before the poem opens, in that its episode giving the earlier events occupies three and a half books of twelve. The chief episode of the *Aeneid,* the hero's narrative of the fall of Troy and his own wanderings, fills but two books of twelve; though that of the *Odyssey* occupies five and a half out of twenty-four, it is still relatively shorter than the angel's narrative in *Paradise Lost.* The *Iliad,* moreover, does not use the method of deliberately narrating events not otherwise included, though slighter use of earlier events occurs. The *Thebaid* of Statius, apparently in Milton's thought when he wrote of "th' Heroic Race . . . That fought at Theb's," is in order of time. So is the *Pharsalia* of Lucan, admired in the seventeenth century.[1] Indeed Statius and Lucan are the only ancients, after Homer and Virgil, mentioned by Davenant in the Preface to *Gondibert.*

Vida's *Christiad,* praised by the youthful Milton,[2] begins late in the life of Jesus and gives a narrative of his early doings. Yet so accomplished a classical scholar as Trissino, writing his *Italia Liberata da Gotti* as a model epic, followed the order of time. Tasso, though using the chronological method,[3] for his classical qualities won the praise of the Aristotelians who censured Ariosto.

In England, Spenser in his Letter to Raleigh explains that "the Methode of a Poet historical is not such, as of an Historiographer. For an Historiographer discourseth of affayres orderly as they were donne, accounting as well the times as the actions; but a Poet thrusteth into the middest, even where it most concerneth him, and there recoursing to the thinges forepaste, and divining of thinges to come, maketh a pleasing Analysis of all." He planned to carry this method so far that his action was to begin with his last book. Yet Davenant, sending out *Gondibert* in 1650, used the order of time. Cowley, however, devotes two of the four completed books of his *Davideis* to narratives of earlier events by Joab and by David himself.

1. E.g., Ben Jonson's notes to the *Masque of Queenes,* "excellent Lucan" (line 55); "Lucan . . . whose admirable verses I can neuer be weary to transcribe" (line 174); "the diuine *Lucan*" (line 179). In the same masque Inigo Jones "chose the *statues* of the most excellent *Poëts,* as *Homer, Virgil, Lucan,* &c. as beeing the substantiall supporters of *Fame*" (lines 684-86). Herrick speaks of "towring *Lucan.*"— *Hesperides,* "The Apparition of His Mistresse Calling Him to Elizium" (ed. Moorman, p. 206). Dante's earlier tributes to Statius (*Purg.,* 21.85-93) and Lucan (*Inf.,* 4.90) are well known.

2. "The Passion," line 26.

3. Such a story from the past as that of Clorinda (12.20-38) is hardly to be considered.

Aristotle does not discuss the matter. Horace, however, writes of the epic poet:

> nec reditum Diomedis ab interitu Meleagri,
> nec gemino bellum Troianum orditur ab ovo;
> semper ad eventum festinat et in medias res
> non secus ac notas auditorem rapit.   (*Ars Poetica*, 146-49)

But how did Milton's time interpret these words? Opinion seems to have rested on that of the Roman commentator Acron:

Semper ad eventum festinat. Scilicet Homerus. Id est, ad id, unde ordiendum est, quod dicunt Graeci: πρὸς τὸ προκείμενον, aut *semper ad eventum festinat,* id est: odit longa prooemia. [ita aperte principia dicit, ut ex iis facile exitus cognoscantur.] Cogitans fastidium lectoris ad exitum operis properat, ideoque non est longius ab origine inchoandum. Sic Ilias Homeri a precibus Chrysae sacerdotis incipit, et Odyssea a concilio deorum. . . . Ita aperte principi adicit, ut ex his media facile noscantur, id est: adducit bonus poeta auditorem [suum] quasi ad nota, hoc est: ita a medietate incipit, quasi superiora nota sint.[4]

---

4. *Acronis et Porphyrionis Commentarii in Q. Horatium Flaccum* ed. Ferdinandus Hauthal (Berlin, 1864), I, 601-2.

Lists compiled by the Bibliothéque Nationale, the British Museum, and the Library of Congress give the following editions of Acron's comment on Horace's *Opera Omnia* or on the *Ars Poetica:* 1471, 1475, 1481, 1485, 1490, 1492, 1494, 1495, 1498, 1499, 1508, 1511, 1512, 1519, 1527, 1528, 1529, 1533, 1536, 1540, 1543, 1544, 1545, 1546, 1553, 1555, 1559, 1562, 1564, 1567, 1568, 1573, 1576, 1580, 1584, 1590. It is not strange, after so many editions of Acron, that Addison gives the *Iliad* as an example of hastening into the midst of things, without reference to the *Odyssey,* though he then speaks of the narrative of Aeneas ("The Fable or Plot," *Spectator,* no. 267).

Acron's work was printed in full in the edition of the *Opera Omnia* by Fabricius (Basle, 1555, 1581). He is mentioned in Francisci Luisini Utinensis *In Librum Q. Horatii Flacci de Arte Poetica Commentarius* (Venetiis, 1554), p. 12. Other commentators who do not mention him, at least in this context, do not controvert his view. See Franciscus Philippus Pedimontius, *Exphrasis in Horatii Flacci Artem Poeticam* (Venetiis, 1546); Vincentius Madius Brixanus, *In Horatii Librum de Arte Poetica Interpretatio* (Venetiis, 1550); Giovanni Fabrini, *L'Opere d'Oratio Commentate* (Venetia, 1573); Iacobus Cruquius, *Q. Horatius Flaccus cum Commentariis . . . Commentatoris Veteris* (Lugduni Batavorum, 1597). Petrus Nannius Alcmarinus comments as follows: "Constat bellum Troianum non aliunde conflatum, quàm è raptu Helenae. plurima tamen omisit, imò ne à

The striking feature of this is that he equates the *Iliad* and the *Odyssey*, with no suggestion that the long narrative of Odysseus at the court of Alcinous, to which no parallel is offered by the short references to the past in the *Iliad,* is vital to the passage in Horace. Similar is the opinion of Vida, who points out that the *Iliad* does not begin with the judgment of Paris, nor the *Odyssey* with the departure from Troy, though he does speak of the narrative of Odysseus at the court of Alcinous.[5] Trissino, a well-informed Aristotelian, even disregarded the idea of the midst of things, declaring in the preface to his *Italia* that he began

dal principio de la detto azione, cioè da l'origine de la guerra, che per tal causa fece co i Gotti. Et in questo ho imitato il divino Omero, il quale volendo descrivere l'ira di Achille, et i danni, che per essa ebbeno i Greci intorno a Troia, cominciò dal principio, et origine de la detta ira, e terminò ne la fine di quella, cioè nel rendere il corpo di Ettore a Priamo.

When the plot of the *Iliad* is the wrath of Achilles rather than the Trojan war, the madness of Achilles and other antecedent actions listed by the Horatians disappear. He further explains that

nel constituire la favola di una azione sola, e grande, e che abbia principio, mezo, e fine, mi sono sforzato servare le regole d'Aristotele, il quale elessi per Maestro, sì come tolsi Omero per Duce, e per Idea.

If Milton were thinking in the terms of the Horatians, a poem beginning with Satan's rebellion could be interpreted as beginning in

raptu quidem incepit Homerus. Nunc videamus, quas res in principio, quas in fine intactas reliquerit poetatum Graecorum princeps: deinde eius rei caussas subnectemus, vt altum summi vatis consilium cognoscamus. Bellum ergo Troianum excitatum, vt dixi, ob raptum Helenae: eum non attigit, vt neque coniurationem procerum in nuptiis Helenes, vbi coniuratum est, vt si quis eam raperet, ceteri vi defenderent. [Then follows a list of various events preparatory to the expedition against Troy, such as the feigned madness of Achilles.] Omnia haec ab Homero praetermissa. Cumque decennio iam decurso bellum durasset, relictis novem annis à decimo exorsus est . . . Quaedam omisit, vt nimium atrocia, qualis erat Iphigeniae immolatio: quaedam vt Heroico carmine indigna . . . Alia omisit vt nimis operosa.— *Commentarius in Artem Poeticam,* in *Q. Horatius Flaccus, cum Erudito Laevini Torrentii Commentario* (Antwerp, 1608).

5. Vida, *Poeticorum Libri,* 2.95. This is well set forth by Macrobius, *Saturnalia* 5.2. Cf. also Quintilian, *Institutes* 7.10.11.

the midst, since an important action is at once treated, with no account of the creation of Heaven or of the Angels, or, according to Milton's theology, of the Son. Nothing is told of earlier thoughts that ripened Satan for action on the very day when the announcement of the Son's headship was made. Yet Milton was an Aristotelian and he had before him his tragic plan for an action limited to the garden. When he turned from that to a poem first giving the proclamation of the Son as king (v. 600), such a beginning seemed remote, even though the Son was to restore happiness to Adam and Eve. If, as will later be suggested,[6] Milton's original plan presented a War in Heaven without the Son, there is the more reason why he should have felt that his *prooemia*, to take Acron's word, were too long. He was not, in the sense of Acron and the other Horatians, beginning in the midst of the events making up his poem, but too early. Satan's plans for attack on man were part of his main story, but the conflict in Heaven that preceded those plans was a little too remote. But when as now the first scene showed Satan ready for his campaign against the newly created world, Milton was beginning in such a way that in the first Argument he could virtually translate Horace's "in medias res . . . auditorem rapit," "the poem hastes into the midst of things."

Milton preferred for his poem the more limited Aristotelian action secured by beginning late. Yet he might have followed the precedent of the *Iliad* or the *Pharsalia* in using chronological order. However much he thought of himself as beginning in the midst of things, the ordinary view of Horatian theory did not require him to adopt,[7] much less to exaggerate, the method of the *Odyssey* by finding a speaker to give a narrative of earlier happenings extending to whole books.

14. Raphael's Narrative of the War in Heaven
(v. 577 - vi. 892)

SEVERAL passages in Raphael's narrative seem inappropriate to the speaker:

6. See Sec. 35, below.
7. For Horatians who distinguished between the method of the *Iliad* as natural and that of the *Odyssey* and the *Aeneid* as artificial, see

Marvin T. Herrick, *The Fusion of Horatian and Aristotelian Literary Criticism, 1531-1555* (Urbana, 1946), pp. 16-20.

> Both addrest for fight
> Unspeakable; for who, though with the tongue
> Of Angels, can relate, or to what things
> Liken on Earth conspicuous, that may lift
> Human imagination to such highth
> Of Godlike Power.[1]   (VI. 296-301)

Is not this by Milton himself, who doubts his own capacity to handle the narrative, as Homer sometimes does?[2] Milton, not Raphael, also seems to speak in the lines on the heroes of the battle:

> I might relate of thousands, and thir names
> Eternize here on Earth; but those elect
> Angels contented with thir fame in Heav'n
> Seek not the praise of men.   (VI. 373-76)

This seems to be the author referring to his own seventeenth century rather than to the time of the Garden of Eden. Further, Raphael tells of his own exploits in the third person, saying:

> Raphael his vaunting foe,
> Though huge, and in a Rock of Diamond Armd,
> Vanquish'd,   (VI. 363-65)

though he has just said he will not tell those of other angels, who desire no glory. To be sure, Julius Caesar always spoke of his military exploits in the third person. Raphael likewise never indicates that he is both speaker and important actor.

To the evidence of these passages that come more suitably from Milton than from Raphael may be added the handling of the narrative itself. The supposed speaker is one of the important seraphs and bore his part in what he relates. Some things he could not have observed, such as what Satan said secretly to Beelzebub (v. 673-93); nor could he have heard Satan's speech to his followers, though Abdiel did hear it. Similarly he could not have known except from Abdiel what that

---

1. Compare:

And thus the Godlike Angel answerd milde	What words or tongue of Seraph can suffice, Or heart of man suffice to com- prehend? (VII. 110-14)
. . . . . to recount Almightie works	Here the words are fitting enough to an angel.

2. *Iliad* 2.488-93.

angel pondered before defying Satan (VI. 113-26). He could not have
been present at the council where the invention of artillery was announced. Apparently when the Devil spoke in derision of the hosts
of Heaven after the discharge of the guns he was heard only by "his
Mates" (VI. 608). Raphael as observer could not have known these
things; they are for an omniscient author. It is true that

> th' Eternal eye, whose sight discernes
> Abstrusest thoughts, from forth his holy Mount
> And from within the golden Lamps that burne
> Nightly before him, saw without thir light
> Rebellion rising, saw in whom.   (v. 711-15)

But at least it is not stated that the Almighty shared all his knowledge
with the heavenly hosts.

Still further, the actions are not told as by a participant. The
angels, though Raphael is one of them, are normally spoken of in the
third person plural. A few of these *they's* are doubtless possible for an
actor, but the majority are those of the historian. They are the more
striking because the first person plural does occur a few times:

> (For wee have also our Eevning and our Morn,
> Wee ours for change delectable, not need);   (v. 628-29)

> . . . though strange to us it seemd
> At first, that Angel should with Angel warr,
> And in fierce hosting meet, who wont to meet
> So oft in Festivals of joy and love
> Unanimous, as sons of one great Sire
> Hymning th'Eternal Father.   (VI. 91-96)

About a hundred lines later there is another first person to mean
Raphael and the other good angels: "Ours joy filld, and shout" (VI.
200). This is in the section on Abdiel, probably an insertion,[3] and the
other so nearly precedes it that it may have been revised when the
insertion was made. In the lines dealing with Abdiel there are no other
pronouns referring to all the good angels. The next instances of the
first person plural occur in a group:

3. See Sec. 37, below.

> Which to our eyes discoverd new and strange,
> A triple mounted row of Pillars laid
> On Wheels. . . . .
> Brass, Iron, Stonie mould, had not thir mouthes
> With hideous orifice gap't on us wide,
> Portending hollow truce; at each behind
> A Seraph stood, and in his hand a Reed
> Stood waving tipt with fire; while we suspense,
> Collected stood within our thoughts amus'd.   (VI. 571-81)

There are no more such uses of the first person until the eighth book is reached. This contains one short passage dealing with the good angels as a body and employing only the first person plural (VIII. 224-46).

There is one passage in the sixth book adapted for narration to Adam; having told of Satan's invention of artillery, Raphael continues:

> Yet haply of thy Race
> In future dayes, if Malice should abound,
> Some one intent on mischief, or inspir'd
> With dev'lish machination might devise
> Like instrument to plague the Sons of men
> For sin, on warr and mutual slaughter bent.   (VI. 501-6)

It must, however, be remembered that if Milton put the angel's books in a new position he adapted them to it, by both revision and addition. The only really characteristic word in the verses just quoted is *thy;* no great change would have been needed to obtain that; or the passage may have been inserted when its present place was given to the story of the War in Heaven.

The conclusion is that the narratives of the fifth and sixth books were not originally composed for Raphael, but were to be given directly by the poet. Then he transferred them to the angel, with a minimum of revision; when he did revise, he thought of the dramatic situation; hence the revised or inserted material had the fitting pronouns. Milton's mingling of persons, suggesting labor on Book VI at different times and with different conceptions, is better evidence of shift in purpose or of stratified composition than any peculiarities in the use of a single person.

15. "That Warning Voice" and Raphael's Visit
(IV. 1-12; V. 219 - VI. 912)

HAVING brought Satan to Mount Niphates, Milton exclaims:

> O for that warning voice, which he who saw
> Th' *Apocalyps*, heard cry in Heaven aloud,
> Then when the Dragon, put to second rout,
> Came furious down to be reveng'd on men,
> *Wo to the inhabitants on Earth!* that now,
> While time was, our first-Parents had bin warnd
> The coming of thir secret foe, and scap'd
> Haply so scap'd his mortal snare; for now
> *Satan*, now first inflam'd with rage, came down,
> The Tempter ere th' Accuser of man-kind,
> To wreck on innocent frail man his loss
> Of that first Battel, and his flight to Hell.   (IV. 1-12)

Such hope for man's escape is out of harmony with the Almighty's assertion that Satan "shall pervert" man (III. 92), and also disregards Raphael's mission; the angel is sent to Adam

> Least wilfully transgressing he pretend
> Surprisal, unadmonisht, unforewarnd.   (V. 244-45)

The conflict of the poet's aspiration with the words of God may be resolved by taking it as merely a wish, but in view of the elaborate warning to come, why should Milton utter it? The most obvious answer is that it was written before the visit of Raphael was planned.

To Milton as a theologian there was no need of more than the Biblical command against tasting the forbidden fruit:

> Quae respicit statum hominis integrum est, qua Deus hominem in horto Edenis collocatum, et ad beate vivendum bonis omnibus instructum, ut esset in quo is obedientiam testatur suam, arbore tantum scientiae boni et mali iussit abstinere.   (*Doct. Chr.* I. 10)

But evidently Milton felt that what was true for theology need not hold for poetry and that his readers might feel that Adam and Eve were not adequately cautioned against the Adversary. Hence the unbiblical visit of the warning angel, wholly unsuggested in the Cambridge Manuscript. It perhaps came in with the plans for an epic.

Its purpose appears in the Almighty's instructions to Raphael for his mission to Adam:

> Such discourse bring on,
> As may advise him of his happie state,
> Happiness in his power left free to will,
> Left to his own free Will, his Will though free,
> Yet mutable; whence warne him to beware
> He swerve not too secure: tell him withall
> His danger, and from whom, what enemie
> Late falln himself from Heav'n, is plotting now
> The fall of others from like state of bliss;
> By violence, no, for that shall be withstood,
> But by deceit and lies. (v. 233-43)

Raphael in the Garden gives a number of lines to free will and to warning (v. 520-43; vi. 893-912; viii. 633-43), but makes no long discourse on the subjects. Nor is much time given to explanation about Satan; he is said to be plotting (vi. 901) but there are no details, nor is there even any mention of "deceit and lies" as his method. It is as though Milton planned a warning with detailed explanation, then rejected it for the long narratives of the Celestial War and the Creation, which merely imply "by dire example" that Adam must be on guard,[1] without indicating that the danger is of "deceit and lies." Adam and Eve know, however, that "sly assault," "fraud," "malice and false guile" (ix. 256, 287, 306) are to be the Devil's chief methods. This knowledge of theirs indicates that the angel did carry out his instructions in full. Violence they do mention, possibly with an echo of "By violence, no," in the divine commission; Eve says:

> His violence thou fearst not, being such,
> As wee, not capable of death or paine,
> Can either not receave, or can repell. (ix. 282-84)

If these words do not echo the charge to the angel, they indicate that Raphael wholly failed to inform the human pair on the kind of danger before them.

The inference from these matters is that Raphael at one time made

---

1. Cf. vii. 42. See also vi. 910.

a relatively short visit, during which he fully carried out his orders to explain about Satan and the coming attack on human bliss. Milton then decided to give the angel the War in Heaven and the Creation. When these were substituted for the short visit, they displaced much of what the angel said in obedience to his divine commission. Still the poet made no change in that commission, though he did feel the need to extend it, for when asked to tell of the Creation Raphael is made to say:

> [What] best may serve
> To glorifie the Maker, and inferr
> Thee also happier, shall not be withheld
> Thy hearing, such Commission from above
> I have receav'd, to answer thy desire
> Of knowledge within bounds.   (VII. 115-20)

This is so evident an afterthought that it leads one to ask why the poet did not turn back to the original commission and insert something of the sort. Without such indications as have just been given, it might be supposed that when Milton decided to carry on his poem in the fashion of the *Odyssey,* by the use of an episodic narrative, he devised the warning as a means for getting an angel into the company of Adam and Eve, thus making Raphael result from the episode rather than the episode from Raphael's presence. The latter implies revision by stages, first Raphael's short warning, then the opportunity of his presence to narrate things unknown to Adam.

16. The Devils
(II. 42-416; V. 671, 695; VI. 357-72, 620-27)

IN THE war in Heaven a number of Satan's followers are named: Adramelec, Asmadai, Ariel, Arioc, Ramiel, Nisroc, Belial, and Moloc, of whom only Belial and Moloc appear in Books I and II, though a number of other devils—Beelzebub, Mammon, and Azazel—are named in addition to those in the muster roll of Satan's forces. Moloc, being called "furious" (VI. 357) and "fiercest" (II. 44), is apparently the same character in both situations; Belial's "gamesome mood" (VI. 620) in Heaven gives no suggestion of his part in the early books. Beelzebub, so prominent in Books I and II, introduced as next to Satan in power

(I. 79), is not named in Books V and VI, though there is an unnamed "next subordinate" (v. 671) who listens and obeys orders. The reader, assuming that this subordinate is Beelzebub, is puzzled that he is nameless and that he lacks color. The two accounts seem to touch each other only in Moloc.

If, however, the War in Heaven preceded the doings in Hell, the situation would be less strange; the nameless subordinate could grow into the stronger Beelzebub without disappointing expectations; Belial would receive in Hell the character not before given him; Moloc would act according to expectation already raised by his part as "furious King" (VI. 357) in Heaven. This condition strengthens the possibility that in an early arrangement Books V and VI were placed before Books I and II.

But even then somewhat more relation between the two accounts might be expected. The lack of it may have come from Milton's method of composing. The War in Heaven, though in his mind when he made the fourth plan for a drama, must as a choral song have been brief. He may have expanded it to the present narrative as soon as his epic determination was confirmed. Books I and II, on the other hand, not being mentioned in the drafts of tragedies, are probably of later planning and composition. After developing them, Milton did not go back to the fifth book to make adjustments. He might have done so had the War in Heaven from the beginning been placed as now,[1] but adjustments were less evidently needed when it came first in the poem. By the time the shift to its present place was made, Milton had become accustomed to the wicked angels as we now have them.

17. The Two Accounts of Satan's Defeat in Heaven
(III. 394-99; VI. 808-88)

AFTER THE Almighty has accepted the Son as the redeemer of man, the angels sing his praise (III. 383 ff.), dealing particularly with his overthrow of Satan at the end of the War in Heaven, described at length in Book VI. The brief account in the third book is much like the longer one in the sixth, even to verbal likenesses:

1. See Sec. 14, above.

> thy flaming Chariot wheels, that shook
> Heav'ns everlasting Frame.   (III. 394-95)

> under his burning Wheeles
> The stedfast Empyrean shook throughout.   (VI. 832-33)

> o're the necks
> Thou drov'st of warring Angels.   (III. 395-96)

> O're Shields and Helmes, and helmed heads he rode
> Of Thrones and mighty Seraphim prostrate.   (VI. 840-41)

> Son of thy Fathers might,
> To execute fierce vengeance on his foes.   (III. 398-99)

> Vengeance is his, or whose he sole appoints.   (VI. 808)

> Victorious King,
> Son, Heir, and Lord, to him Dominion giv'n,
> Worthiest to Reign.   (VI. 886-88)

Extolling "with loud acclaime" (III. 397) is not verbally suggested in Book VI, but the angels do celebrate Messiah's triumph. The first two pairs of quotations use little Biblical language, and the concept of Satan and his followers overthrown by the Son rather than by Michael is not a usual one. No one on a first reading of *Paradise Lost* would suppose that Milton intended the Son to take part in the expulsion of Satan; hence such a reader would not be prepared for the references in Book III. The brief account does not give the effect of having been written when the fuller one was not yet planned but rather, as a hymn celebrating the Son's exploits, seems to imply the longer one, even containing the words "thou that day" (III. 392). The repetition, then, is deliberate. But nevertheless its effect is curious because, since the reader does not yet know the account in Book VI, the details are not familiar. It may be accounted for by supposing that in an early ar- ·rangement the War in Heaven preceded Book III. In such a sequence the reader of the hymn of triumph would already know the narrative on which it depends.

18. How Books V and VI Fitted into Book I
(I. 27-49; V. 577 - VI. 877)

THE ARGUMENT tells that Book I "touches the prime cause of his fall,
the Serpent, or rather Satan in the Serpent; who revolting from God,
and drawing to his side many Legions of Angels, was by the command
of God driven out of Heaven with all his Crew into the great Deep."
The verse gives but fourteen lines (36-49) for so much summary.
As though realizing this, Milton continues in the Argument: "Which
action past over, the Poem hasts into the midst of things"; he then
proceeds to mention the scene in Hell which is fully given in the verse.
Why did Milton so carefully specify the passing over and the hastening into the midst of things? The answer is found in his process of
composition.

The part of the Argument first quoted might serve not as a summary of a few lines but of the whole War in Heaven, now occupying
a book and a half, but probably shorter in Milton's earlier plans.[1] The
wording would not be impossible if instead of line twenty-seven, immediately following the poet's introductory statement of purpose,
there were a verse now much later in the poem,

> As yet this world was not, and Chaos wilde,   (v. 577)

and if the narrative of the celestial war continued from that point to
the overthrow of Satan into Hell:

> Hell at last
> Yawning receavd them whole, and on them clos'd,
> Hell thir fit habitation fraught with fire
> Unquenchable, the house of woe and paine.   (VI. 874-77)

After this would come what is now in the first book:

> Nine times the Space that measures Day and Night
> To mortal men, he with his horrid crew
> Lay vanquisht,   (I. 50 ff.)

and then for a space the poem would continue as now.

1. In Sections 35 and 37 I give reasons for thinking that in early
versions Books V and VI said little about the Son and nothing
about Abdiel.

It seems, then, that Milton decided after much reflection, perhaps after some experiment, to break up such an early chronological order. Lifting the War in Heaven from its first position, he gave it to Raphael, revising some of the lines to fit their new place, and discarding much of the first account of the angel's mission. But then he had a problem at the beginning of his poem. The body of the work, following the introduction, began at line 27, with

Nine times the Space that measures Day and Night.

(I. 50)

But this was not self-explanatory. Homer could depend on pronouns in the eleventh line of his *Odyssey* because he had already mentioned Troy and by paraphrase his hero. Vergil, making a complete break, in his twelfth verse began his account of Carthage. Milton had not mentioned Satan in his account of his subject. Like Vergil, he must name him and tell where he is. But Milton went beyond that, giving a summary of the rebellion in Heaven, with even a few lines (44-48) that parallel a larger number near the end of Book VI (864-77). Though our "Grand Parents" are mentioned, lines 27-49 are chiefly concerned with the secondary matter of Satan's rebellion, and introduce Book I rather than the poem as a whole. Moreover, though the verses themselves may be praised, the total effect of this summary is awkward. A little of it might have gone with "loss of Eden" in the first statement, but this second and longer statement of part of the subject is not wholly assimilated; it seems to show Milton over-supplying what was needed, namely that the Infernal Serpent is lying in Hell after his fall from Heaven. It is strange that the poet did not more carefully work out lines so conspicuous; did he for once leave a passage because it was successful in itself, even though not wholly adapted to its setting?

After the removal of the War in Heaven, some change in the Argument was required. It may be that the War was already represented by the words: "Satan . . . who revolting from God, and drawing to his side many Legions of Angels, was by the command of God driven out of Heaven with all his Crew into the great Deep." If so, they were left unchanged,[2] though applying only to a dozen lines. The

---

2. Except in tense, though the past does occur at least once elsewhere in the Arguments.

succeeding words were then added: "Which action past over, the Poem hasts into the midst of things." *Past over* seems to mean *hurried over*, as is done in the summary of Lucifer's revolt, contrasting with the full account it supplanted; the words almost imply a time when the earlier events were not "past over," when the poet had not so fully observed Horace's precept "ad eventum festinat."[3] That the poem hastened into the midst of things was still more important for Milton. He may have moved the angelic rebellion because he was dissatisfied with his first arrangement; with his Aristotelian desire for a limited action, he felt that his story stretched too far. When his solution came, with its plunge *in medias res*, and its opening scene on the Lake of Fire, he had what he had wished for. In his happiness over his success, he wrote the explanation—unnecessary to the argument—of the Odyssey-like plunge into the middle of the story.

In earlier sections, it has been shown that the visit of Raphael may have come late into the poem and that the War in Heaven was not written to be narrated by him but apparently by the poet himself. If not told by the angel, it could hardly have been in the midst of the poem. Now it appears that a few rough bricks at another part of the building suggest that it once was attached to them. There seems, then, reason to believe that the first form of *Paradise Lost* began with the War in Heaven, in other words, that the early part of the poem at one time stood in chronological order.

The end of the War in Heaven, whether brought about by Michael and his angels, or by Messiah, must be the utter defeat of the rebels. Milton tells how they were

> Exhausted, spiritless, afflicted, fall'n,

and that the Son

> as a Heard
> Of Goats or timerous flock together throngd
> Drove them before him Thunder-struck.   (VI. 852-58)

If Messiah had taken no part, the rout might have been more in the tone of the account of the first day's fight:

> Gabriel . . .
> . . . with fierce Ensignes pierc'd the deep array

3. *Ars Poetica*, line 148. See Sec. 13, above.

> Of *Moloc* furious King, who him defi'd,
> And at his Chariot wheeles to drag him bound
> Threatn'd, nor from the Holie One of Heav'n
> Refrein'd his tongue blasphemous; but anon
> Down clov'n to the waste, with shatterd Armes
> And uncouth paine fled bellowing.[4]   (VI. 355-62)

Moloc is not merely represented as completely defeated but also as made ridiculous.[5]

Had Milton continued his chronological arrangement, a reader would have gone from such passages to the spectacle of Satan lying chained in impotence on the burning lake, with his helpless followers around him. In contrast with his defeat immediately preceding, the proud speeches of the "confounded" Satan would more evidently have deserved the author's comment:

> Vaunting aloud, but rackt with deep despare,   (I. 126)

and that the Devil's "high words" bore "semblance of worth, not substance" (I. 529). Even lines 27-49, commented on as unduly long,[6] perhaps find their explanation in an attempt by Milton to retain at the beginning of the poem something of the effect of Satan's bad qualities and weakness; he is, for example, ambitious to set himself in glory above his peers, and at last is hurled down "with hideous ruin." But however this may be, the removal of the detailed story of his expulsion from Heaven made it easier for readers to interpret Satan as a powerful adversary of the Miltonic God.

4. Cf. the defeat of the bad by the good angels in Vondel's *Lucifer*, Act V, lines 1727-1981.
5. See Allan H. Gilbert, "A Parallel between Milton and Boiardo," *Italica*, XX (1943), 132-34.
6. Above, in this section.

CHAPTER FIVE

THE MIDDLE EPIC SHIFT OF THE CREATION

19. The Parting Angel and the Original Position of Book VIII
(VI. 894-912; VIII. 630-32, 652-53; IX. 274-78)

IN THE course of her difference with Adam over their work in the Garden, Eve says:

> That such an Enemie we have, who seeks
> Our ruin, both by thee informd I learne,
> And from the parting Angel over-heard
> As in a shadie nook I stood behind,
> Just then returnd at shut of Evening Flours.   (IX. 274-78)

The Angel departed at sunset, as the eighth book tells (line 630), after spending with Adam the half day prescribed by the Almighty.[1] In that book, however, he gives no caution against Satan, but only one against passion; in the seventh there is a warning (lines 542-47), but not associated with the departure of the angel. To what can Eve refer?

At the end of the sixth book, having finished the War in Heaven, Raphael concludes:

>   That thou maist beware
> By what is past, to thee I have reveal'd
> What might have else to human Race bin hid:
> The discord which befel, and Warr in Heav'n
> Among th' Angelic Powers, and the deep fall
> Of those too high aspiring, who rebelld
> With Satan, hee who envies now thy state,

---

1. v. 229. Cf. VII. 98-108.

> Who now is plotting how he may seduce
> Thee also from obedience, that with him
> Bereavd of happiness thou maist partake
> His punishment, Eternal miserie;
> Which would be all his solace and revenge,
> As a despite don against the most High,
> Thee once to gaine Companion of his woe.
> But list'n not to his Temptations, warne
> Thy weaker; let it profit thee to have heard
> By terrible Example the reward
> Of disobedience; firm they might have stood,
> Yet fell; remember, and fear to transgress.   (VI. 894-912)

This seems to be the warning mentioned by Eve, once immediately followed by the departure of the angel at evening. At that time Book VII was not in its present place. Indeed, as has been shown,[2] that book is not warranted by a strict interpretation of the Almighty's original charge to Raphael (v. 229-45), but only by the angel's addition that he was to answer Adam's "desire of knowledge" (VII. 119-20). Eve's statement that she overheard the warning when she returned in the evening would then apply to the passage quoted, which evidently assumes her absence, because of the words, "Warn thy weaker." Yet as the poem now stands she does not leave Adam and Raphael until later, at the beginning of the eighth book, so that she hears the admonition in company with Adam. Hence the proper thing for her to say in the ninth book is: "I know that we have such an adversary, for I heard the caution as you did." But since she says she only overheard Raphael, her departure must originally have been before the angel began to tell of the War in Heaven, or even earlier, perhaps when they had finished their meal, and

> Sudden mind arose
> In Adam, not to let th' occasion pass
> Given him by this great Conference to know
> Of things above his World, and of thir being
> Who dwell in Heav'n.   (v. 452-56)

As we have seen, the celestial conflict in Books V and VI was not originally related by the angel.[3] Hence his departure before that narra-

2. Sec. 15, above.   3. Sec. 14, above.

tive was put in his mouth must have been earlier in the fifth book than the present beginning of his long narrative (line 563). Eve's retirement would then have come before the warning, and the passage last quoted might be equivalent to the "studious thoughts abstruse" (VIII. 40) that, as the poem now stands, lead her to rise from her seat and go to attend to her flowers.[4] There may have then followed the account of Eve's creation, Adam's avowal of admiration for her, and the angel's counsel against excessive love that now comes near the end of Book VIII (465-611, 633-43). Combined with this or following it was the warning against Satan with which Raphael was charged by the Almighty. As has been said,[5] the Argument of Book V includes in that book the warning against the "enemy" and the Argument of Book VI disregards its presence in the concluding lines of that book. Apparently the Argument of Book V preserves Milton's original intention. According to the early plan, the angel departed after the warning, just as Eve returned.

When Raphael's hypothetical short account of Satan, ending with admonition against him, was omitted in favor of the long story of the War in Heaven, the warning words were properly put at the conclusion of Book VI, where Raphael's visit then ended. On deciding to prolong the angel's stay, Milton added Book VII and Book VIII, at the end of which Raphael now departs. When this was done, the warning overheard by the returning Eve should have been moved to the end of Book VIII. This could not have been done without combining it with the counsel against passion that now comes near the end, or making some other change. Indeed the present conclusion is perhaps just enough like the required warning against Satan to have given Milton the sense that he had done what his structure required. Eve's later reference to her overhearing (IX. 276) now remains to indicate the additions Milton made to his original plan for the angelic visit.

"The creation of Eve with thire love, & mariage," now in Book Eight, appears in the fourth plan for a tragedy;[6] it may also have appeared in the fifth. In the early form of the epic this topic may have been included in the relatively brief conversation of Raphael and

4. Sec. 48, below.
5. Sec. 3, above.

6. See Milton's Plan for a Tragedy, Act I, in Sec. 2, above, and Fig. 2.

Adam; presumably it concluded with the angel's caution against excessive love for Eve, to the loss of self-control, that now comes near the end of Book VIII (561-94). It was followed by the warning against Satan (now VI. 908-12) and the angel's departure, as evening came on (IX. 278). Then Milton interposed the War in Heaven and the Creation between the advice against passionate love and the Fall. After that, wishing the caution against excessive love for Eve to precede as closely as possible the Fall that was to result from that love, Milton put the material of Book VIII in its present place, forgetting, however, that the warning against Satan's wiles should also be transferred to Raphael's departure. Not until he shifted the book did he write its astronomical beginning, which easily follows the cosmology of Book VII. Even with that addition it is an unusually short book, as though the matter at hand was limited.[7]

It seems, then, that, except perhaps in Plan Five, the part of Book VIII relating to Eve has always been episodic, and always part of Adam's narrative to the angel. Its change in place, after two books and a half were inserted between it and Book IX, was only for the purpose of bringing it again close to the story of the Fall.

20. Who Are Meant by *their?*
(III. 59)

AFTER ITS introductory portion the third book continues:

> Now had the Almighty Father from above,
> From the pure Empyrean where he sits
> High Thron'd above all highth, bent down his eye,
> His own works and their works at once to view. (III. 56-9)

What of his own works has he in mind? The most likely answer is the newly created world, often so referred to, as in the morning hymn of Adam and Eve:

> These are thy glorious works, Parent of good.   (V. 153)

7. Book VII is shorter by thirteen lines and Book XII by four. The subject of VII is limited and XII was made by dividing one book that originally contained XI as well. Books VII, VIII and XII are each more than two hundred lines below the average of the poem (themselves included).

In the seventh book, as is fitting because it deals with the Creation, there are several such references to *works*. The scene at the beginning of the third book is that God, in the Empyrean "High Thron'd above all highth" with the Son on his right (III. 58-64), is looking down on the world just made; the Argument puts it: "God sitting on his Throne sees Satan flying toward this world, then newly created." The situation, save for the looking down, is that at the end of the Creation:

> At the holy mount
> Of Heav'ns high-seated top, th' Impereal Throne
> Of Godhead, fixt for ever firm and sure,
> The Filial Power arriv'd, and sate him down
> With his great Father.   (VII. 584-88)

The hymn then sung by the angels mentions toward its end man as ruling "over his Works" (VII. 629). The Almighty needs but to look, and the first scene of Book III is before us, as though that book followed the seventh. But as the poem now stands, in the first two books there has been reference to God's works only by Beelzebub. If, however, the third book followed the seventh, the reference to the Creation would be pertinent.

What, however, are "their works"? The only beings other than God to whom works are attributed in *Paradise Lost* are man, Nature, and Satan. Satan is mentioned in the same paragraph. A singular pronoun would naturally apply to him; does the plural apply to him and his followers? Apparently *their works* are quite distinct from the works of God.[1] At any rate the early part of the third book appears not to have been fully adjusted to some change or omission.

21. The Two Accounts of the Creation of the World
(III. 708-32; VII. 224-386)

URIEL GIVES the disguised Satan a summary account of the first, second, and fourth days of Creation, dealing especially, as befits the

---

1. The poem gives no reason to believe that *their* refers to man, as though the Almighty were inspecting what his creatures had done. Man's daily work was, however, "appointed" (IV. 618, 726), "enjoyn'd," "assignd," or "impos'd" (IX. 207, 231, 235) by God. If once there were a scene, preceding the third book, in which God looked down to see how man was carrying out his duties, it has now vanished.

angel of the Sun, with light and the heavenly bodies. There is little verbal similarity between his words and the extended narrative in Book VII except for the "borrowed" (III. 730; VII. 377) light of the moon, but the ideas are much the same, as in the reference to the boundary of the universe.[1] Uriel, indicating the enclosing shell of the world, says:

> The rest in circuit walles this Universe.   (III. 721)

In the story of Satan's voyage we have already read how he landed

> upon the firm opacous Globe
> Of this round World, whose first convex divides
> The luminous inferior Orbs.   (III. 418-20)

Though the notion of such a protective shell would have been intelligible to many of Milton's contemporaries, these references are clearer after reading the formal account of the Creation given by Raphael, who tells of the circumscription of the world by the divine compasses and speaks of the "just Circumference," the "hollow Universal Orb" (VII. 231, 257), and

> the uttermost convex
> Of this great Round: partition firm and sure.   (VII. 266-67)

The use of different ideas in detail, as the moon with "countenance triform" (III. 730), and "less bright" (VII. 375), and the choice of matter pertinent only to Uriel leave little doubt that the story of Creation is repeated deliberately. The brief and selective recital is, however, better fitted to follow than to precede the long and inclusive one. So far as the account in Book III implies knowledge of that in Book VII, it suggests that in Milton's early arrangement Book VII preceded Book III.

22. The Two Narratives of Adam's Creation
(VII. 519-50; VIII. 203-356)

ADAM'S CREATION is related twice. First, it appears in the Six Days as they are set forth by Raphael in Book VII, where it is on the same

---

1. See Gilbert, "The Outside Shell of Milton's World," *Studies in*   *Philology*, XX (1923), 444-47; and McColley, *op. cit.*, p. 129.

scale as the other days. Like the rest of the chronicle of Creation, it is taken from Genesis 1, with the addition of the warning to Adam from Genesis 2:16, 17. Second, in the eighth book, Adam, following the second chapter of Genesis, describes his own beginning. He prefaces his story with these words, among others:

> Thee I have heard relating what was don
> Ere my remembrance: now hear mee relate
> My Storie, which perhaps thou hast not heard. (VIII. 203-5)

Most of what the angel related was before Adam's remembrance, but not the latter part of the Sixth Day, as Raphael himself had pointed out, using the expressions "thou know'st," and "thou remember'st" (VII. 561). Yet soon he contradicts himself by saying to Adam, on completing the Creation: I have told

> what before thy memorie was don
> From the beginning.   (VII. 637-38)

If these words remain from a time when Raphael gave a brief account of Satan's revolt and other early matters, now displaced by much of Books V, VI, and VII, the contradiction is explained. Book VII is so obvious a well-proportioned hexameral narrative that it can never have broken off at the point where Adam's memory begins.

At any rate, Raphael gladly hears Adam's story, especially because, as he says: "I that day was absent" (VIII. 229). The "day" of his absence is not explained; we know that it was the Sixth of Creation only from what comes after. It seems likely that at some time the "day" was specified, but that the passage was dropped in the course of revision. If Raphael was absent, he could not have observed the Sixth Day of Creation, and must have been obliged to relate it to Adam only at second hand, as common knowledge in Heaven. Not merely in his narrative of the Creation does Raphael show knowledge of events on the day of his absence, but in telling of the War in Heaven, he explains the array of the angels with the comparison:

> As when the total kind
> Of Birds in orderly array on wing
> Came summond over Eden to receive
> Thir names of thee.   (VI. 73-76)

Perhaps much stress should not be laid on an illustration as a sign of stratified composition. So far as it may be taken seriously, either it must have been written before Milton had the angel explain his absence, or the poet had forgotten that explanation. The image itself may have been written when Book VI was shifted and adapted to its new place or may have resulted from later revision.

With more reason it can be said of the seventh book as a whole that only in forgetfulness can it have been assigned to Raphael after his absence had been asserted. On the other hand, would the author, soon after putting the narrative of the Sixth Day in Raphael's mouth, have proceeded to write Raphael's disclaimer of knowledge? Since that disclaimer is more likely to be overlooked than is the entire seventh book, one may suppose that the reason for his willingness to listen to Adam was written early enough to have become dim in Milton's brain before he put the narrative of Creation in its present place and wrote the simile in Book VI.

If the poet had wished to avoid inconsistency, his plan for a narrative of Creation in which all the days are treated on the same scale might have been abandoned and the latter part of the Sixth given to Adam, who was present, rather than to the angel, who was not. But then the dialogue on astronomy now at the beginning of the eighth book would have made a break between the angel's warning against excessive love and the exhibition of that love in Book IX. Milton did not undertake the labor of substituting Adam's narrative of man's creation for the angel's and of finding another position for his contrast of the old and the new astronomy.

23. The Fruit Forbidden
(IV. 421-24; VII. 542-47; VIII. 323-35)

ONE OF THE first things said by Adam to Eve is that God had required of them only

> This one, this easie charge, of all the Trees
> In Paradise that bear delicious fruit
> So various, not to taste that onely Tree
> Of knowledge.   (IV. 421-24)

When Raphael joins the caution: "If ye be found obedient" (v. 501, 513-14, 522), there is no need to mention the tree; everybody knows it is indicated. Again, though included by the angel under the words "as thou know'st" (vii. 536), the prohibition is repeated from Genesis 2:17 as part of the account of the Sixth Day of Creation, which, as has been said, Raphael did not himself witness (viii. 229). In telling of his own early experience, Adam again repeats God's forbidding of the fruit (viii. 323-35). Since in the preceding book Raphael had set this forth, it seems natural that Adam should remark on its being familiar to his visitor, but he makes no indication that it is less novel than other parts of his discourse. This adds another to the suggestions of lack of harmony between Books VII and VIII that already have been given, and thus is a further indication that Book VII came late to its present position.

In the dialogue of the eighth book the effect is almost as though Milton took a tragic scene, worked the stage directions into the text, and added *replied* and similar words to the names of speakers. As highly dramatic material, partly included in Plan Four, and close to the central weakness or tragic flaw of Adam, part of Book VIII probably was designed for the tragedy of Plan Five. If so, it is earlier than Book VII, which can only pertain to Milton's epic plans. When Milton gave the seventh book to Raphael, he put it in the form of a narrative addressed to Adam, but forgot that portions of the eighth book also needed to be adapted to the knowledge that the angel, as teller of the story of Creation, necessarily possessed.

24. Did Book VII Once Precede Book III?
(vii. 131-38)

VARIOUS DETAILS in Book VII adapt it to narration by Raphael. The pronouns in the third person plural applied to the angels are not disturbing, though *our* rather than *their* might have been used in line 138, and *we* rather than *they* in 565. Raphael more than once specifically addresses Adam: "for of Armies thou hast heard" (vii. 296);

> Thou thir Natures know'st, & gav'st them Names,
> Needless to thee repeated; nor unknown
> The Serpent suttl'st Beast of all the field,

. . . . though to thee
Not noxious, but obedient at thy call   (VII. 493-98)

When he comes to Adam's own creation he addresses him directly
and adds the warning against the forbidden fruit (VII. 524-47). He
reminds his auditor of the angelic harmonies (VII. 561) heard at the
end of the Sixth Day, and remembers him in a comparison describing
Heaven: the pavement of the road to God's house is made of stars,

As Starrs to thee appeer,
Seen in the Galaxie, that Milkie way
Which nightly as a circling Zone thou seest
Pouderd with Starrs.   (VII. 578-81)

Yet the book as a whole is not personal to the speaker. It is essentially
a set piece such as a poet might base on Genesis without thought of
dramatic possibility, and the appeals to Adam are evident inserts that
do not change its total effect.

Obviously the introductory portion (VII. 1-39) was written for
its specific place and that place was such that Milton could write:
"Half yet remains unsung" (VII. 21), even though when *Paradise Lost*
was first published in ten books the seventh, already bearing that
number, was followed by only three. If the *barbarous dissonance* of
line 32 is correctly interpreted as referring to the Restoration, these
initial lines must have been composed after the King came back. But
to date them is not to date the remainder of the book; as we have seen,[1]
there is some reason to think them an insertion. It seems likely, then,
that the seventh book came late to its present place.

On its earlier position some hints have been noted, especially the
Almighty's mention of "his own works" near the beginning of Book
III.[2] If Book VII directly preceded Book III, it can hardly have been
placed elsewhere than immediately following the present Book II.
That book carries Satan's voyage to his first sight of the universe of
man; Book III shows his actual arrival in it. Having brought Satan
through Chaos, and within sight of the "pendant world" (II. 1052),
the poet might have asked, "What is this world that Satan saw?" and
then described its creation. Or, omitting the four lines referring to

1. See Sec. 3, above.   2. See Sec. 20, above.

the universe, he might have written *Meanwhile* or some sign of epic transition, and continued:

> After *Lucifer* from Heav'n
> (So call him, brighter once amidst the Host
> Of Angels, then that Starr the Starrs among)
> Fell with his flaming Legions through the Deep
> Into his place, and the great Son returnd
> Victorious with his Saints, th'Omnipotent
> Eternal Father from his Throne beheld
> Thir multitude, and to his Son thus spake.   (VII. 131-38)

The Father then would explain his plan for creating man to take the place left vacant by the fallen angels and at once proceed to the Creation. After that he could look down on the Adversary still in Chaos (III. 70), and the globe of the world would be ready for Satan to alight on when he arrived (III. 422).

25. The Early Arrangement of *Paradise Lost*

WHEN MILTON decided to write an epic, he was obliged to make additions to dramatic material already partly or wholly shaped. He also had before him the problem of epic rather than dramatic order. The preceding sections have shown something of what went on as he worked. Now there is presented, by way of summary, the arrangement posited for the poem in its earliest state; it is not to be thought of as at any time solidified in this precise form; the process of building was continuous and the relation of the various changes cannot be fixed. For example, the story of Abdiel may have been inserted into the War in Heaven before the latter was moved from its initial position;[1] the War may have been shifted before the bulk of Books I and II were written; many other modifications can be imagined, though traces of them seem not to have remained. For the sake of simplicity only large sections are usually listed.[2]

1. See Sec. 37, below.
2. For example, in Book II, lines 629-48 should probably be included in Satan's voyage. In the table in Section 50 more detail has been attempted.

THE MATERIAL OF *Paradise Lost* AND ITS ARRANGEMENT
BEFORE THE SHIFT FROM CHRONOLOGICAL ORDER

(In the right-hand column are passages not then included)

BOOK I

Lines 1-40. Invocation
and statement of sub-
ject.

BOOK V

Lines 694-802. War in
Heaven.

Without Abdiel (803-end).
Without the Son as the cause of revolt
(577-693); Pride given as the cause.

BOOK VI

Lines 44-107, 205-669.
War in Heaven.

Without Abdiel (1-44, 107-202).
Without Messiah's victory (669-892);
victory by the angels followed line 669.

BOOK I

Lines 50-669. Satan's
host in Hell.

Without Pandaemonium and the council
therein (670-end), but with a council in
the field.

BOOK II

Lines 884-1055. Satan's
voyage.

Without the council (1-520).
Without the amusements of the devils
(521-628).
Without Sin and Death (648-884).

BOOK VII

Lines 131-634. Crea-
tion.

Without the introduction (1-130) and not
addressed to Adam.

BOOK III

Lines 56-92, 250-65.
Council in Heaven.

Without the introduction (1-55).
Without free will, divine foreknowledge,
and the Redemption (93-249, 266-415).

Lines 418-end. Satan in
the Sun.

BOOK IV

Lines 1-775. Satan in the Garden; Adam and Eve.

Without the arrest of Satan (776-end).

BOOK V

Lines 1-543. Raphael's visit.

BOOK VIII

Lines 198-643. Adam's narrative to Raphael.

Without astronomy (1-197).

BOOK VI

Lines 895-912. Warning to Adam against Satan.

BOOK IX

Lines 48-end. The Fall.

Without the introduction (1-47).

BOOK X

Lines 1-228. Judgment.
Lines 649-end. Sufferings of Adam and Eve; quarrel, penitence.

Without Sin and Death (229-418, 585-640).
Without Hell (418-584).

BOOK XI

Lines 1-71. Redemption.
Lines 72-end. Michael's visit to Adam.

BOOK XII

Lines 1-end. Michael's visit and the expulsion from the Garden.

Such an epic would have been short; the passages suggested amount to almost 7,000 lines, or about two-thirds the present length of the poem. In addition, it would have included passages for which substitutes were afterwards provided and probably sections later omitted without leaving a trace. It would probably still have been shorter than the *Aeneid,* which is somewhat shorter than the finished *Paradise Lost.*[3]

It may be repeated that the scheme given above is only approximate. When something like its arrangement was contemplated, Milton was still working on the poem and was unsettled about many things. Certain topics indicated as lacking were perhaps already there; for example, the victory of the Messiah over Satan may already have been introduced into Book VI. On the other hand, some themes may not yet have been dealt with, as Satan's meeting with Uriel. Nor can the line numbers be taken as other than a general guide to the early form, since much revision intervened between the period of chronological order and the completion of the manuscript. Especially at the points where transferred or new material was inserted there must have been much rewriting. Yet, though the table brings into settled form what probably never existed as a whole and at a single moment, it still gives a picture of Milton at work.

The chronological order was not satisfactory to him, for reasons evident to one who imagines the effect of the hypothetical poem in comparison with that of the finished *Paradise Lost.* Half the work is over before man appears; the human action all comes in one block. The order of time gives a leisurely effect instead of the intensity Milton desired. Variety he highly esteemed, for

variety (as both Musick and Rhethorick teacheth us) erects and rouses an Auditory, like the maisterfull running over many Cords and divisions; whereas if men should ever bee thumming the drone of one plaine Song, it would bee a dull Opiat to the most wakefull attention.[4]

The early order does not secure the variety coming from a rapid succession of different scenes and characters.

The solution was Raphael's narrative, putting the War in Heaven in the midst of the epic. Its action being thus "past over," as the Argument of Book I has it, the poem had a striking first scene, and the block of material derived from the dramas had been cleft. But still the poem

3. The *Aeneid* is of 9895 lines, *Paradise Lost* of 10565.
4. *Animadversions upon the Remon-strants Defence against Smectymnuus,* sec. 2, p. 27 (Columbia ed., III, 133).

was too slow in arriving at the Garden. The seventh book was then assigned to Raphael, where it received in Adam's curiosity a new motive. Now man appeared sufficiently early, though still after he had been prepared for in both Hell and Heaven. In its new place the descriptive seventh book contrasted with the less solemn activity before and after it, and yet did not retard the action as when it was interposed in Satan's voyage. The shift of this book also enabled Milton to introduce Adam's scientific interest. The poem, though unfinished, now had the order we know.

CHAPTER SIX

LATE EPIC MATERIAL

26. Satan Seeks Further Knowledge of Adam and Eve
(IV. 528-33)

THE Argument of Book IV tells how Satan, after overhearing Adam tell Eve of the forbidden fruit, plans to found his temptation on it and "then leaves them a while, to know further of thir state by some other means." The verses themselves add a reference to chance but do not much expand the Argument:

> But first with narrow search I must walk round
> This Garden, and no corner leave unspi'd;
> A chance but chance may lead where I may meet
> Some wandring Spirit of Heav'n, by Fountain side,
> Or in thick shade retir'd, from him to draw
> What further would be learnt.   (IV. 528-33)

These two passages lead to the expectation that Satan will find some spirit to question as he questioned Uriel in the Sun. But there is no further reference to his search; he next appears at Eve's ear in the form of a toad. What did he wish to know? Whether the Garden is patrolled by angels? It seems that at some time there must have been in Milton's plan an incident that made Argument and verses necessary. Is it possible that the warning later given to Gabriel by Uriel may once have been given instead by an angel earlier encountered by Satan in the Garden itself?

27. Satan as a Toad and Eve's Dream
(IV. 797-856; V. 28-135)

IN DRAFT FOUR it is said that Lucifer "seeks revenge on man the Chorus prepare resistance at his first approach."[1] Apparently he approaches the chorus of his own initiative. This is quite unlike the situation in the epic, where two angels, Ithuriel and Zephon, search the Garden and at last find him

> Squat like a Toad, close at the eare of *Eve;*
> Assaying by his Devilish art to reach
> The Organs of her Fancie, and with them forge
> Illusions as he list, Phantasms and Dreams,
> Or if, inspiring venom, he might taint
> Th'animal Spirits that from pure blood arise
> Like gentle breaths from Rivers pure, thence raise
> At least distemperd, discontented thoughts,
> Vaine hopes, vaine aimes, inordinate desires
> Blown up with high conceits ingendring pride.   (IV. 800-9)

Touching the Fiend with his spear, Ithuriel restores him to his normal shape. Satan is unabashed:

> Know ye not then said *Satan,* fill'd with scorn,
> Know ye not mee? ye knew me once no mate
> For you, there sitting where ye durst not soare;
> Not to know mee argues your selves unknown,
> The lowest of your throng; or if ye know,
> Why ask ye, and superfluous begin
> Your message, like to end as much in vain?   (IV. 827-33)

Zephon, "answering scorn with scorn," replies that Satan's appearance is now as foul as is Hell his place of doom. It is possible, though not necessary, to find here something of the "discourse of enmity" of Milton's fourth draft.

But though Milton's early plans may appear in these speeches, the description of Satan's attempt on Eve must be later. It can have been written only after Milton decided to give something on life in the Garden before the Fall. Even the tragedy mentioned by Phillips can hardly have contained it, because the action involving Satan in the

1. See Milton's Plan for a Tragedy, Act II, in Sec. 2, above, and Fig. 2.

form of a toad, suddenly restored to his normal form, is hardly possible on the stage. Unless assigned in drama to some narrator, it must have been written after the epic form was settled upon. Eve's dream itself, however, being necessarily a matter of narrative, could have been part of a drama.

The Arguments of Books IV and V imply, and one normally supposes, that the dream Eve relates was inspired by Satan. There is, however, no such statement in the text. Moreover, the dream, while not setting Eve among the gods, ends calmly, though suddenly, and allows her to sink down and fall asleep (v. 92); yet Satan is apparently disturbed in the midst of his operations at her ear. In addition, while he does attempt to forge dreams, he also hopes to inspire "venom" to raise discontent and pride;[2] the latter is more prominent in the passage quoted above than are dreams. Even the word *dreams* is a vague plural; if this passage and the dream of the next book had been planned as one action, would not a specific dream have been mentioned, after the manner of Homer?[3] Possibly something, though but little, of the results of Satan's "venom" appears in Eve when she wishes to leave Adam on the day of the Temptation; she has pride enough to expect to overcome Satan, but not more.[4] Moreover in the description of Satan's activity at the ear of Eve, he is not reported as successful; he is "assaying" or striving to reach her fancy or to taint her animal spirits with venom, but there is no indication that he succeeded, except in the Argument, which plainly says "tempting her in a dream," with no reference to phantasms or animal spirits. So far as the text goes, there is only a vague connection between Satan's work as the toad and Eve's dream or her overconfidence in meeting trial alone; it is hardly possible that the activity of Satan and Eve's subsequent experience and conduct were planned at one time as a continuous action.

One may suppose that first the attempt of Satan was devised, in the course of developing the search for revenge on man mentioned in Plan Four,[5] but without any immediate outcome. Later the dream

2. See Murray W. Bundy, "Eve's Dream and the Temptation in *Paradise Lost*," *Research Studies of the State College of Washington*, X (1942), p. 278.

3. *Iliad*, 2.16-22.

4. IX. 384. The Argument of Book IX speaks of Eve as "the rather desirous to make tryal of her strength."

5. See Milton's Plan for a Tragedy, Act II, in Sec. 2, above, and Fig. 2.

itself was planned as an insertion.[6] In the first section of the fifth book Adam admires the beauty of the sleeping Eve. Into the midst of this passage are thrust three lines:

> so much the more
> His wonder was to find unwakn'd *Eve*
> With Tresses discompos'd, and glowing Cheek,
> As through unquiet rest.   (v. 8-11)

This is not quite in the tone of the remainder of the passage. He wakens her by telling how the "fresh field" calls them to see the beauties painted by Nature. Then comes the dream and Adam's learned explanation. The earlier situation is resumed with the words: "To the field they haste" (v. 136). There is not thereafter the slightest reference to Eve's dream, though it would have been natural for her to allude to it when Satan in his interview with her produced a parallel. It appears that the arguments of Books Four and Five were adjusted to the insertion of the dream,[7] since they give more effect of continuity than does the text. Book IV itself, however, was not adjusted, perhaps through forgetfulness that it did not say that Satan succeeded and that it gave to tainting of the animal spirits more weight than to dreams.

A further hint that Satan's metamorphoses into a cormorant,[8] into a lion and a tiger and other animals (IV. 397-408), and then into a toad came late into the poem may be derived from the circumstances of his later transformation into a serpent. The Arch-Fiend does not welcome the necessity laid upon him:

> O foul descent! that I who erst contended
> With Gods to sit the highest, am now constraind
> Into a Beast, and mixt with bestial slime,
> This essence to incarnate and imbrute,
> That to the hight of Deitie aspir'd.   (IX. 163-67)

There is here no suggestion that this is not the first metamorphosis into an animal. Moreover, the serpent into which the Tempter entered was exceedingly beautiful, far superior to the toad, though perhaps not to

6. For insertion in *Comus*, see Fig. 4.
7. See Sec. 3, above.
8. The text merely says "sat like a cormorant" (IV. 196), the Argument "in the shape of a Cormorant." When he leaves the tree his disguise is unmentioned (IV. 396).

the lion. At least it might have been expected that Satan's lament would have accompanied an early transformation rather than the last one in the Garden. That, as part of the Biblical story, Milton necessarily had in mind from the beginning. Even if the serpent did not actually appear in the tragedy mentioned by Phillips, Satan may there have announced his plan, with his loathing of the serpentine disguise it involved. The other disguises are not essential and all are epic; at least none of them could have been considered for the stage except as narrated. It seems that all may be of later date than Satan's expression of disgust at imbruting the essence that aspired to deity.

28. Satan's Outward Lustre
(I. 94-97; IV. 835-40, 849-50; VI. 394-97)

WHEN SATAN was found by Ithuriel and Zephon

> Squat like a Toad, close at the eare of Eve,   (IV. 800)

Ithuriel touched him with his spear. Since under the touch of "Celestial temper," all falsehood returns to its own likeness, the Fiend "started up in his own shape." The two angels had supposedly been familiar with his appearance in Heaven, yet they do not recognize him, for they ask:

> Which of those rebell Spirits adjudg'd to Hell
> Com'st thou?

Satan, fill'd with scorn, answers:

> Know ye not then . . . . .
> Know ye not mee? ye knew me once no mate
> For you, there sitting where ye durst not soare;
> Not to know mee argues your selves unknown,
> The lowest of your throng; or if ye know,
> Why ask ye? . . . . . .
> To whom thus Zephon, answering scorn with scorn.
> Think not, revolted Spirit, thy shape the same,
> Or undiminisht brightness, to be known
> As when thou stoodst in Heav'n upright and pure;
> That Glorie then, when thou no more wast good,
> Departed from thee, and thou resembl'st now
> Thy sin and place of doom obscure and foule.   (IV. 827-40)

On hearing this the Devil stood abash't "and pin'd His loss" of good-
ness and virtue,

> but chiefly to find here observd
> His lustre visibly impar'd.   (iv. 849-50)

How is this to be interpreted? Are the angels, when they ask Satan
who he is, merely rhetorical, or are they really in doubt? Satan does
not actually name himself, but after his speech beginning "Know ye
not," are not names superfluous? The angels know that only one can
talk like that. If their question is not merely scornful, they do not
recognize Satan because he is changed; moreover Satan, expecting to
be recognized, does not realize that his lustre is visibly impaired. If so,
Milton's word *find* ("to find here observd His lustre visibly impar'd")
is to be taken in the most obvious sense, so that the phrase means *to
learn for the first time that his lustre is so diminished that observers
know it.* The only test of impaired lustre is whether it is evident to
observers; the angels see that it is impaired; hence it is.

Satan had earlier accepted such a change in himself, contrasting it
with his unimpaired firmness of mind:

> Yet not for those,
> Nor what the Potent Victor in his rage
> Can else inflict, do I repent or change,
> Though chang'd in outward lustre.   (i. 94-97)

He insists on his "unconquerable will" and the "strength undiminisht"
of his followers. Yet he sees that they too have diminished in splendor;
Satan has addressed Beelzebub:

> If thou beest he; But O how fall'n! how chang'd
> From him, who in the happy Realms of Light
> Cloth'd with transcendent brightness didst out-shine
> Myriads though bright.[1]

Satan's claim of unimpaired strength is true, even when tested by
the events of the War in Heaven. To be sure the leader himself and
many of his followers are wounded and

> Then first with fear surpris'd and sense of paine
> Fled ignominious, to such evil brought

1. i. 84-87. Cf. ii. 305.

> By sin of disobedience, till that hour
> Not liable to fear or flight or paine;   (VI. 394-97)

on the other hand, the angels who have not sinned are recognized by
Nisroc as "unpaind, impassive" (VI. 455). The Almighty explains why
Michael and his powers do not conquer the rebels:

> Equal in their Creation they were form'd,
> Save what sin hath impaird, which yet hath wrought
> Insensibly, for I suspend thir doom.   (VI. 690-92)

The word *insensibly* seems hardly to fit the "bellowing" of the
wounded Moloc (VI. 362), yet the strength of the rebel angels is such
that they sustain the conflict. Later Satan admits his failing powers,
because of which he is unwilling to undertake conflict with Adam,

> Whose higher intellectual more I shun,
> And strength, of courage hautie, and of limb
> Heroic built, though of terrestrial mould,
> Foe not informidable, exempt from wound,
> I not; so much hath Hell debas'd, and paine
> Infeebl'd me, to what I was in Heav'n.[2]   (IX. 483-88)

Satan's inconsistencies about his failing lustre and his unfailing
might are apparently a result of stratified composition. The scenes in
Hell appeared early in Milton's epic writing; it is poetically effective
that Satan should appear as an archangel, though ruined. When still
later Milton inserted the episode of Ithuriel and Zephon, the effect to
be obtained from the proud Adversary's ignorance of his own decay
was not to be neglected. Possibly, having in mind Satan's early assertion of unflagging demoniac strength, Milton forgot that he had written an admission of change in outward glory.

29. The Position of Hell and Heaven
(II. 884-920; VII. 210-14)

IN THE Argument of Book I, Milton makes clear that he puts Hell "not
in the Center (for Heaven and Earth may be suppos'd as yet not made,
certainly not yet accurst) but in a place of utter darknesse fitliest call'd

2. Satan also admits that he dreads   same as dreading conflict with
   the vigilance of the guardians of   them.
   Paradise (IX. 158); this is not the

Chaos."[1] Such a position of Hell, remote from the universe of man, is also argued for in the *De Doctrina Christiana*, 1.32. As early as *The Doctrine and Discipline of Divorce*, Milton wrote of

a locall hell, whether in the aire[2] or in the center, or in that uttermost and bottomlesse gulph of *Chaos*, deeper from holy blisse then the worlds diameter multiply'd (Chap. III, Columbia ed., III, 442).

The word *deeper* indicates situation below, and in *Paradise Lost* it is said that Satan and his followers have fallen into a Hell

> As far remov'd from God and light of Heav'n
> As from the Center thrice to th' utmost Pole.[3] (I. 73-74)

Many passages support the view that Hell is below and the Empyreal Heaven above. In *Paradise Lost* this Heaven where God especially shows forth the glory and splendor of his majesty is apart from the universe of man and above Chaos. In the *Christian Doctrine* Milton supports the same view, though with the caution that he lays down no rule on it,[4] thus making clear that such matters in the epic do not demand literal belief. The universe of man, not far from Heaven, is once represented as hanging from it by a golden chain (II. 1051). According to this normal scheme, Satan's followers fall from Heaven and when they go to the Earth their course is upward.

But this is not invariably true. Though Satan once says:

1. Two exceptions have been pointed out; one is

In Heaven, or Earth, or under Earth in Hell. (III. 322)

This is obviously the ordinary underground Hell, probably mentioned by mere inadvertence. The other is "the mouth of hell" (XII. 42); it obviously means *called the mouth of hell;* see Gilbert, *Geographical Dictionary of Milton*, p. 43.

2. This possibility is also touched in *Paradise Lost*, x. 185-89; XII. 454-55 (cf. *Paradise Regained*, I. 39-46; II. 117).

3. This means three times as far as from the center of the universe to the celestial pole. In the prose quotation above, *world* means *universe.*—See Gilbert, "The Outside Shell of Milton's World," *Studies in Philology*, XX (1923), 444-47. Literally, the distance is absurd, for beside Chaos the universe is very small, as appears throughout Satan's journey, so that Hell is remote from Heaven by thousands of world-diameters. Milton has taken a unit of measurement that means *great beyond imagination* and applied it to Chaos with that meaning, not the literal one.—See B. A. Wright, "Masson's Diagram of Milton's Spaces," *Review of English Studies*, XXI (1945), 42-44.

4. I. 7 (Columbia ed., XV, 29-31).

Gates of burning Adamant
Barr'd over us prohibit all egress,   (II. 436-37)

as though it were necessary to rise directly upward to escape, the
gates of Hell are also differently presented. When Satan approaches
them

At last appeer
Hell bounds high reaching to the horrid Roof,
And thrice threefold the Gates; . . . .
. . . . . Before the Gates there sat
On either side a formidable shape.   (II. 643-49)

When Sin is about to open the gates, she raises the portcullis, and then

The Gates wide op'n stood,
That with extended wings a Bannerd Host
Under spread Ensigns marching might pass through
With Horse and Chariots rankt in loose array;
So wide they stood, and like a Furnace mouth
Cast forth redounding smoak and ruddy flame.
Before thir eyes in sudden view appear
The secrets of the hoarie deep, a dark
Illimitable Ocean without bound
. . . .
Into this wild Abyss the warie fiend
Stood on the brink of Hell and look'd a while,
Pondering his Voyage; for no narrow frith
He had to cross.   (II. 884-920)

Hell is in this passage a land bordering on the ocean of Chaos. When
Satan actually begins his journey, it is as confused as the materials of
Chaos. He uses both foot and wing, though on the whole he goes up-
ward, until at last he sees the World hanging down from Heaven.

When the Creation is to be, the Creator and his hosts come forth
from the gates of Heaven:

On heav'nly ground they stood, and from the shore
They view'd the vast immeasurable Abyss
Outrageous as a Sea, dark, wasteful, wilde,
Up from the bottom turn'd by furious windes
And surging waves.   (VII. 210-14)

Here too Chaos seems to be the ocean on the shore of Heaven. Sin
and Death build their bridge, as a bridge must be, over rather than

through Chaos (II. 1026; X. 253, 257, 301, 309, 314, 370), and Satan meets them at its foot, on the outside of the World; yet it gives a passage "down" to Hell (X. 305, 414), on which Satan "descends" (X. 394). Even the World once becomes a "happy Ile" (II. 410) as though off the coast of Heaven. It is evident, then, that while Heaven is usually above and Hell below, Milton does not hesitate to use language that puts them virtually on a level. This suggests that his scheme is figurative and poetical rather than factual and necessary.

The placing of Hell on a level with Chaos is entirely a matter of the sections where Sin and Death appear. If this part of the second book had been written consecutively with the preceding matter, it is less likely that an unconventional view of the position of Hell would have been used. But if the allegory was composed separately and inserted in Book II, divergence is more to be expected. The section on the children of Satan in Book X, presumably later than that in Book II,[5] almost of necessity continues the episode as it was begun in the earlier book.

In Book VII the Creator goes out into Chaos as Satan did, but with a contrasted purpose; he intends "good out of evil to create" (VII. 188) and

> to create
> Is greater then created to destroy. (VII. 606-7)

It seems likely that the similar situation but contrasted purpose must have been in Milton's mind and that he intended the reader to observe it. The seventh book is an episode, not vital to the plot, while Satan must issue from Hell in order to tempt man. But whether the Creator's view of Chaos as an ocean or Satan's similar view was first written is less important than that they seem related. If in the original order of the books, Book VII immediately followed II,[6] the contrast and likeness of the two views of Chaos would be more apparent than now.

30. Hell as Pit and Universe
(I. 91, etc.; II. 58, etc.; X. 418-66)

A HELL in the limitless Chaos may easily deserve to be called a world (II. 262, 572), a universe (II. 622), within which are all earthly features

5. See Sec. 38.   6. See Secs. 24 and 20, above.

made horrible, seas (I. 300), plains, hills, rivers, continents. Pandaemonium is in a ₊ˡain (I. 350, 700), "many a dark League" (x. 438)
from the borders of the kingdom.

But Milton also speaks quite differently. Hell is a den (II. 58), a
pit (I. 91, 381, 657; II. 850; IV. 965; x. 464) and, as in Revelation 20:3,
the bottomless pit (VI. 866), a house of pain (II. 823; VI. 877), and a
dungeon (I. 61; II. 1003; x. 466). These words indicating a relatively
limited space, even a confined one, may be supposed derived from
the usual view of Hell as within the Earth. Yet it may be recalled that
Dante's upper circles are spacious, and that Tasso has plenty of room
for an assembly of devils in an underground Hell from which they
depart "fuor volando a riveder le stelle" (4.18).

Since the words indicating limited extent are Scriptural, they are,
according to Milton's views of Biblical interpretation,[1] harmonious
with his view that Hell is extra-mundane. Indeed in the *Christian
Doctrine* (1.33) the New Testament expressions *fornax ignis* (Matt.
13:42) and *puteus abyssi* (Apoc. 21:8) occur in the paragraph preceding that in which Hell is set *extra hunc mundum*. Yet in Book II
the two types of word are not intermingled. When the devils are
prisoners or lament their misery, Scriptural words indicating small
spaces, such as *dungeon*, are used. When the demons explore Hell,
the concept employed is that of great extent; yet its words are not
from the Bible; they can be justified only by reasoning that a Hell
in limitless Chaos could be of huge size. If Milton wrote for his
tragedies passages in which Hell is mentioned, the usual conception
of Hell as a pit would probably have prevailed, if only because he
would not have had space to set forth any other notion. In *Samson
Agonistes* any difficulty is passed over by taking the belief of the

---

1. For Milton and his theological
contemporaries, every passage of
Scripture—no matter how it
seems to us—was in harmony with
their views; to admit that any
passage was against them would
have been to abandon their position. This was true of men of all
the varying beliefs. Hence Milton felt at liberty to use any
Biblical language, putting on it

his own interpretation, though
aware that readers holding different views would take it to
mean something different. Interpreters in the present day, then,
can never assume that what seems
to them the plain meaning of
Biblical words used in *Paradise
Lost* has any relation to the significance Milton himself saw
there.

Gentiles who "condemn to thir abyss" those who do not keep divine secrets (line 500). Some of the expressions of vast space in *Paradise Lost* occur in sections that for other reasons seem to be of late composition.[2]

31. The Devils in Council
(I. 752 - II. 505)

BELIAL IS mentioned in Book I, in the catalogue of Satan's followers, as a lewd spirit "gross to love Vice for it self" (I. 491-92). Lust, violence, luxury, riot, outrage, insolence, and drunkenness are associated with him. This is not the same picture as of the Belial who speaks in Satan's council. There he is

> in act more graceful and humane;
> A fairer person lost not Heav'n; he seemd
> For dignity compos'd and high exploit:
> But all was false and hollow; though his Tongue
> Dropt Manna, and could make the worse appear
> The better reason, to perplex and dash
> Maturest Counsels: for his thoughts were low;
> To vice industrious, but to Nobler deeds
> Timorous and slothful: yet he pleas'd the ear,
> And with perswasive accent thus began.   (II. 109-18)

About the only suggestion of this in the earlier picture is that he loved "Vice for it self." Moloc also appears as one of the leaders of Satan's host. While his descriptions there and at council are less far apart than the two of Belial, yet there is no sense of relation between them. Beelzebub, though Satan's "bold compeer," is a less impressive figure in Book I than in Book II. His first speech, notwithstanding a vigorous line or two, is so despairing as to deserve in answer:

> Fall'n Cherube, to be weak is miserable
> Doing or Suffering.   (I. 157-58)

His next, though showing fear of the Omnipotent, is flattery of Satan in the assurance that if his legions hear his voice, "they will soon resume New courage and revive" (I. 278-79). Though more than his merely

2. See Secs. 32, 39, 50 (Group VI).

listening part when Satan begins his rebellion,[1] this is less than that of
the Beelzebub who, though still a tool,

> in his rising seem'd
> A Pillar of State; deep on his Front engraven
> Deliberation sat and public care;
> And Princely counsel in his face yet shon,
> Majestic though in ruin: sage he stood
> With *Atlantean* shoulders fit to bear
> The weight of mightiest Monarchies; his look
> Drew audience and attention still as Night
> Or Summers Noon-tide air.   (II. 301-9)

Perhaps there is comic intention here, since Beelzebub, like some
modern politicians, looks his part too well, though he plays his rôle
ably. How did Milton come to make these differences in the same
characters, as they appear in Book I and in Book II? The question
virtually is: Were the two books composed as a unit?

There is further reason to think they were not. When addressing
his forces after they have been mustered, Satan, in spite of his pride
in the number of his warlike followers, yet tells them that henceforth
they will not provoke "new warr,"[2] but, abandoning force, work "by
fraud, or guile" and suggests one possibility for its employment:

> Space may produce new Worlds; whereof so rife
> There went a fame in Heav'n that he ere long
> Intended to create, and therein plant
> A generation, whom his choice regard
> Should favour equal to the Sons of Heaven:
> Thither, if but to pry, shall be perhaps
> Our first eruption.   (I. 650-56)

Though the procedure of the devils seems here settled as trickery, the
Argument of Book II says that "Satan debates whether another Battel
be to be hazarded for the recovery of Heaven." Satan himself does not
quite do that, though he does say they are sure to recover their old
inheritance

---

1. v. 672. See Sec. 16, above.
2. Earlier he had declared that he
   would "wage by force or guile

eternal Warr" (I. 121) and later
he declares for "Warr open or
understood" (I. 661-62).

> and by what best way,
> Whether of open Warr or covert guile,
> We now debate, (II. 40-42)

as though he had not already decided on "fraud or guile" (I. 646). Secondly, in the council in Hell, Beelzebub proposes an attack on man as something unknown to his audience:

> What if we find
> Some easier enterprize? There is a place
> (If ancient and prophetic fame in Heav'n
> Err not) another World, the happy seat
> Of som new Race call'd *Man*, about this time
> To be created. . . . .
> Thither let us bend all our thoughts, to learn
> What creatures there inhabit, of what mould,
> Or Substance, how endu'd, and what thir Power,
> And where thir weakness, how attempted best,
> By force or suttlety. . . . . . .
> . . . . . . this place may lye expos'd
> The utmost border of his Kingdom, left
> To their defence who hold it: here perhaps
> Some advantagious act may be achiev'd
> By sudden onset, either with Hell fire
> To waste his whole Creation, or possess
> All as our own, and drive as we were driven,
> The punie habitants, or if not drive,
> Seduce them to our Party. (II. 344-68)

When the speech is over, Milton comments

> Thus Beelzebub
> Pleaded his devilish Counsel, first devis'd
> By Satan, and in part propos'd, (II. 378-80)

but this shows that Milton realized the idea had appeared before rather than makes Beelzebub's words a reference to something already known. Though Satan's earlier proposal is mentioned in the Argument, the total effect is that Milton in Book I had Satan both propose the attack on man, as Tasso's Satan proposes that on the crusaders,[3] and then

---

3. *Gerusalemme Liberata*, 4.9-17.

proceed to carry it out. This is further confirmed by the Argument of that book, which runs:

Satan . . . tells them lastly of a new World and new kind of Creature to be created, according to an ancient Prophesie or report in Heaven; . . . *for that Angels were long before this visible Creation, was the opinion of many ancient Fathers.* To find out the truth of this Prophesie, and what to determin thereon he refers to a full Councel. What his Associates thence attempt. Pandemonium the Palace of Satan rises, suddenly built out of the Deep.

Thence seems to mean either *afterward* or *as a result*, but there is no result from a council. Nor do the devils merely attempt anything; they actually accomplish the building of Pandemonium, "easily" and "in an hour" (1. 696-97). In five lines (1. 650-54) Satan tells of the world and man, and there is no immediate council and no endeavor "to find out the truth." The Argument fits a condition in which the matter was at once considered and Satan's followers, not merely the Adversary himself, as now, proceeded to action.[4] In an early stage of the poem, this council in Book I probably was described soon after Satan brought forward his plan for attacking man (about 1. 669), and then came a decision on the conduct of the fallen angels and some action by them perhaps connected with Satan's offer to undertake the voyage, now in the second book (lines 426 ff.).

Then Milton had the inspiration for the council that now stands in the poem, founded on his own observation of public life as well as on his reading, and giving a picture of Satan as a modern political boss, for the council is a satire of the weaknesses of representative government. The poet seems to have developed it for its own sake with great pleasure and with little thought of its connection with other parts of his poem, except in the character of Satan. Yet the council as it is fits the spirit of the rest of the work, and though it makes this part of the epic disproportionately long, its brilliancy hides the lack of balance.

The whole situation, from the state of the Arguments to the independent development of the character of the speakers, suggests that this council is an interpolation so late that Milton's time for full revision was limited. Possibly this accounts for the failure of the Argument of

4. See Sec. 3, above.

Book II to mention even the names of the four carefully developed speakers, much less to give a summary of their speeches.

32. Pandaemonium
(i. 670-764; x. 422-44)

AFTER HAVING mustered his legions in Hell, Satan addresses them and they applaud with enthusiasm. Milton then abruptly writes: "There stod a hill not far," and the building of the palace of Pandaemonium has begun. There are no words of transition.[1] After the account of the structure and its architect, the poem immediately continues:

> Meanwhile the winged Haralds by command
> Of Sovran power, with awful Ceremony
> And Trumpets sound throughout the Host proclaim
> A solemn Councel forthwith to be held
> At Pandaemonium, the high Capital
> Of Satan and his Peers.　　　　　(i. 752-57)

The palace has not before been named. It is strange both that the name comes indirectly in this fashion and that the sentence runs as though the palace were known but had not been described immediately before. This condition, taken with the lack of correspondence between Argument and text,[2] suggests that at one time there was other material here or a different arrangement; perhaps the attempt of Satan's associates mentioned in the Argument was related.

In the Argument of Book I, Pandaemonium is called the "palace of Satan." The account of its rise from the earth seems also to make it a single structure (i. 722-23, etc.), and it is compared with temples or palaces in Babylon and Alcairo. According to the received texts, it is called Satan's "high capital" (i. 756). In the manuscript of the first book, however, the word was first written *capitol* and the *o* was changed to *a*. Miss Darbishire, examining the matter, holds that *capitol* is unquestionably right and that the change was made by an "officious corrector."[3] Her ground essentially is that Milton presents a building

---

1. For Milton's views on transition see his *Logic*, 2.17 (Columbia ed., Vol. XI).
2. See Sec. 3, above.

3. *The Manuscript of Milton's Paradise Lost, Book I*, ed. Helen Darbishire (Oxford, 1931), p. 68. See also pp. xxiii and xxv.

but not a city. Not until the tenth book is Pandaemonium again mentioned. There it is called the "citie and proud seate of Lucifer"
(X. 424-25), and his metropolis (X. 439). Yet certainty is still lacking,
for it is also a "Plutonian Hall" (X. 444, 522). In both accounts the
privates remain in the field outside the building (I. 758; X. 533); those
of higher rank are in the hall (I. 762; X. 453); the great Seraphic Lords
and Cherubim are in a room far within (I. 792-94; X. 456-57).

It seems that Milton intended both a city and a palace, but the relation of the two is not now evident. Doubtless the matter was clear in
the poet's own mind and perhaps at one time clear in what he had
written. If at an early stage in the composing, Satan's followers
debated their attack on man immediately after their muster,[4] the palace
would have had no function as a meeting-place. Since, too, the description is an ornamental passage and episodic, it probably was composed
later than the remainder of Book I.

33. The Plan of Salvation
(III. 144-371; XI. 22-44; XII. 395-551)

IN MILTON's fourth plan for a tragedy, almost at the end, come the
words: "Mercy comforts him promises the Messiah." Building on this
dramatic basis, though substituting Michael for Mercy, Milton in the
eleventh and twelfth books developed this comfort to Adam through
the Savior and the plan of Salvation. In the third book the same material is gone over. In the epic Milton could include a scene in heaven
such as he was unwilling to use in tragedy. The Son offers to satisfy
justice by taking over the guilt of man and is approved by the Father.

There are similaries in the two accounts:

> He with his whole posteritie must dye,
> Dye hee or Justice must.   (III. 209-10)

>   . . . nor can this be,
> But by fulfilling that which thou didst want,
> Obedience to the Law of God, impos'd
> On penaltie of death, and suffering death,
> The penaltie to thy transgression due,

4. See Sec. 31, above.

And due to theirs which out of thine will grow:
So onely can high Justice rest appaid.   (XII. 395-401)

The Son offers himself:

Behold mee then, mee for him, life for life
I offer, on mee let thine anger fall;
Account mee man; I for his sake will leave
Thy bosom.   (III. 236-39)

                              Let mee
Interpret for him, mee his Advocate
And propitiation, all his works on mee
Good or not good ingraft, my Merit those
Shall perfet, and for these my Death shall pay.
Accept me, and in mee from these receave
The smell of peace toward Mankinde, let him live
Before thee reconcil'd.   (XI. 32-39)

          On me let Death wreck all his rage;
Under his gloomie power I shall not long
Lie vanquisht; thou hast givn me to possess
Life in my self for ever, by thee I live,
Though now to Death I yield, and am his due
All that of me can die, yet that debt paid,
Thou wilt not leave me in the loathsom grave
His prey, nor suffer my unspotted Soule
For ever with corruption there to dwell;
But I shall rise Victorious, and subdue
My vanquisher, spoild of his vanted spoile;
Death his deaths wound shall then receive, and stoop
Inglorious, of his mortall sting disarm'd.
I through the ample Air in Triumph high
Shall lead Hell Captive maugre Hell, and show
The powers of darkness bound.   (III. 241-56)

          Death over him no power
Shall long usurp; ere the third dawning light
Returne, the Starres of Morn shall see him rise
Out of his grave. . . . . . .
. . . . . this God-like act
Annuls thy doom, the death thou shouldst have dy'd,.

In sin for ever lost from life; this act
Shall bruise the head of *Satan,* crush his strength
Defeating Sin and Death, his two maine armes,

. . . .

Then to the Heav'n of Heav'ns he shall ascend
With victory, triumphing through the aire
Over his foes and thine; there shall surprise
The Serpent, Prince of aire, and drag in Chaines
Through all his Realme, and there confounded leave.

(XII. 420-55)

The working of the plan is explained:

His crime makes guiltie all his Sons, thy merit
Imputed shall absolve them who renounce
Thir own both righteous and unrighteous deeds,
And live in thee transplanted.   (III. 290-93)

See Father, what first fruits on Earth are sprung
From thy implanted Grace in Man. . . . .
. . . . . all his works on mee
Good or not good ingraft.   (XI. 22-35)

                    His obedience
Imputed becomes theirs by Faith.   (XII. 408-9)

                    Thy Humiliation shall exalt
With thee thy Manhood also to this Throne;
Here shalt thou sit incarnate, here shalt Reign
Both God and Man, Son both of God and Man,
Anointed universal King, all Power
I give thee, reign for ever, and assume
Thy Merits; under thee as Head Supream
Thrones, Princedoms, Powers, Dominions I reduce:
All knees to thee shall bow.   (III. 313-21)

Then enter into glory, and resume
His Seat at Gods right hand, exalted high
Above all names in Heav'n.   (XII. 456-58)

The living, and forthwith the cited dead
Of all past Ages to the general Doom
Shall hast'n, such a peal shall rouse thir sleep.
Then all thy Saints assembl'd, thou shalt judge

Bad men and Angels, they arraignd shall sink
Beneath thy Sentence; Hell, her numbers full,
Thenceforth shall be for ever shut. Mean while
The World shall burn, and from her ashes spring
New Heav'n and Earth, wherein the just shall dwell.

(III. 327-35)

Thence shall come,
When this worlds disolution shall be ripe,
With glory and power to judge both quick and dead,
To judge th' unfaithful dead, but to reward
His faithful, and receave them into bliss,
Whether in Heav'n or Earth, for then the Earth
Shall all be Paradise. (XII. 458-64)

It is to be expected that ideas of so great moment to Milton should
be repeated, and that he would be obliged to make use of consecrated
formulas; still, in spite of that, more variation would probably have
been given if the passages had been planned to complement each other.
It is true that Michael's speeches in the twelfth book are addressed
to Adam, who did not know of the council in Heaven; yet they are
also addressed by Milton to his readers. The scene in Heaven at the
beginning of the eleventh book (lines 14-125) is, however, not written
for Adam's hearing, but is a direct report by Milton to the reader of
what was said by Father and Son. Had it been composed with the
council of Book III in mind, it would have been a claiming of the
promise already made by the Father:

Be thou in *Adams* room
The Head of all mankind, though *Adams* Son.
As in him perish all men, so in thee
As from a second root shall be restor'd,
As many as are restor'd, without thee none.
His crime makes guiltie all his Sons, thy merit
Imputed shall absolve them who renounce
Thir own both righteous and unrighteous deeds,
And live in thee transplanted, and from thee
Receive new life. So Man, as is most just,
Shall satisfie for Man, be judg'd and die,
And dying rise, and rising with him raise
His Brethren, ransomd with his own dear life. (III. 285-97)

But in Book XI the Son makes his petition:

> Let mee
> Interpret for him, mee his Advocate
> And propitiation, all his works on mee
> Good or not good ingraft, my Merit those
> Shall perfet, and for these my Death shall pay.
> Accept me.   (XI. 32-37)

The Father grants the Son's request. It is evident that if Book III had been clearly in the poet's mind when he was composing Book XI, the Son would have said to the Father that now he claims the promise already made, but as the poem stands the scene in Book XI seems a shorter duplicate of that in Book III, and is unrelated to it.

The scene in Book III is presumably later than those in Books XI and XII, because the passages found in the last two books were already in Milton's mind when he was making the notes in the Cambridge Manuscript. The function of the theology in the first half of Book III is not to add anything new to *Paradise Lost* but to give the utmost force to a central idea by bringing the Plan of Salvation into the action at an early and critical point, so that before Satan begins his seduction of man the reader sees him as powerless to do other than follow the divine will. Such a function, implying a full view of the completed poem, suggests the heavenly dialogue in Book III as written when the main scheme of the epic was complete. Milton can hardly have been unaware that he had repeated this important theme—probably desired to do so—but he did fail to make in the later books adjustments to the equivalent material presented in the earlier one.

34. Free Will

(III. 95-128; V. 233-37, 524-40; VIII. 635-37; IX. 351-52; X. 43-47)

THE ARGUMENT of Book V tells how "God to render Man inexcusable sends Raphael to admonish him of his obedience, of his free estate, of his enemy near at hand." This is given more fully in the Almighty's charge to the angel:

> Such discourse bring on,
> As may advise him of his happie state,

> Happiness in his power left free to will,
> Left to his own free Will, his Will though free,
> Yet mutable.   (v. 233-37)

The angel carries out his charge:

> God made thee perfet, not immutable;
> And good he made thee, but to persevere
> He left it in thy power, ordained thy will
> By nature free, not over-rul'd by Fate
> Inextricable, or strict necessity;
> Our voluntarie service he requires,
> Not our necesitated, such with him
> Findes no acceptance, nor can find, for how
> Can hearts, not free, be tri'd whether they serve
> Willing or no, who will but what they must
> By Destinie, and can no other choose?
> My self and all th' Angelic Host that stand
> In sight of God enthron'd, our happie state
> Hold, as you yours, while our obedience holds;
> On other surety none; freely we serve,
> Because wee freely love, as in our will
> To love or not; in this we stand or fall.   (v. 524-40)

It is also touched on in the angel's caution just before he departs:

> Take heed least Passion sway
> Thy Judgement to do aught, which else free Will
> Would not admit.   (viii. 635-37)

This favorite idea of Milton's appears elsewhere, as when Adam explains to Eve

> God left free the Will, for what obeyes
> Reason, is free, and Reason he made right,   (ix. 351-52)

and when the Almighty declares that man fell

> no Decree of mine
> Concurring to necessitate his Fall,
> Or touch with lightest moment of impulse
> His free Will, to her own inclining left
> In eevn scale.   (x. 43-47)

The most striking passage on the subject is prepared for by the
Argument of Book III: "God . . . foretells the success of Satan in
perverting mankind; clears his own Justice and Wisdom from all
imputation, having created Man free and able enough to have with-
stood his Tempter." The verses run:

>   So will fall,
> Hee and his faithless Progenie: whose fault?
> Whose but his own? ingrate, he had of mee
> All he could have; I made him just and right,
> Sufficient to have stood, though free to fall.
> Such I created all th' Ethereal Powers
> And Spirits, both them who stood and them who faild;
> Freely they stood who stood, and fell who fell.
> Not free, what proof could they have givn sincere
> Of true allegiance, constant Faith or Love,
> Where onely what they needs must do, appeard,
> Not what they would? what praise could they receive?
> What pleasure I from such obedience paid,
> When Will and Reason (Reason also is choice)
> Useless and vain, of freedom both despoild,
> Made passive both, had servd necessitie,
> Not mee. They therefore as to right belongd,
> So were created, nor can justly accuse
> Thir maker, or thir making, or thir Fate,
> As if predestination over-rul'd
> Thir will, dispos'd by absolute Decree
> Or high foreknowledge; they themselves decreed
> Thir own revolt, not I: if I foreknew,
> Foreknowledge had no influence on their fault,
> Which had no less prov'd certain unforeknown.
> So without least impulse or shadow of Fate,
> Or aught by me immutablie foreseen,
> They trespass, Authors to themselves in all
> Both what they judge and what they choose; for so
> I formd them free, and free they must remain,
> Till they enthrall themselves: I else must change
> Thir nature, and revoke the high Decree
> Unchangeable, Eternal, which ordain'd
> Thir freedom, they themselves ordain'd thir fall.
>
>   (III. 95-128)

For this elaborate passage there is no suggestion in Plan Four, though in Plan Three the debate in the first act between Justice, Mercy, and Wisdom would have permitted something of the sort, since, as Milton indicates (III. 132-34), man's use of his free will brought about the display of both divine Mercy and divine Justice. Plan Five would assuredly have contained this theme of free will as it is now developed in the informing words of Raphael quoted above (v. 524-40). When Milton rewrote his drama as an epic, then, he would have had ready to hand a speech on his favorite topic of freedom. But still he was not satisfied with its exposition. There then appeared to him the opportunity offered by the third book, in which he had dramatically arranged to present the Father as foiling Satan before his work began. In addition to the way of Redemption, he could include also a more eloquent exposition of human free will and divine foreknowledge than he had yet written. This part of the theology of the third book, since it is not indispensable to the story and repeats what is said elsewhere, is presumably a late addition to the epic. The passage in itself, where the poet attains a vigor in the expression of his purpose that hitherto had been lacking, is one of the important achievements of his revision.

35. Messiah Anointed and Victorious
(III. 315-21; V. 600-6)

THE EXCITING cause of Satan's revolt is a speech by the Almighty:

> Hear all ye Angels, Progenie of Light,
> Thrones, Dominations, Princedoms, Vertues, Powers,
> Hear my Decree, which unrevok't shall stand.
> This day I have begot whom I declare
> My onely Son, and on this holy Hill
> Him have anointed, whom ye now behold
> At my right hand; your Head I him appoint.   (v. 600-6)

But in the third book also the Son assumes the office of Mediator; in accepting him the Father declares:

> Here shalt thou sit incarnate, here shalt Reign
> Both God and Man, Son both of God and Man,
> Anointed universal King, all Power

> I give thee, reign for ever, and assume
> Thy Merits; under thee as Head Supream
> Thrones, Princedoms, Powers, Dominions I reduce:
> All knees to thee shall bow.   (III. 315-21)

Are these two equivalent proclamations, one of which, would have disappeared in perfect revision?

On the figurative begetting of the Son, the *Christian Doctrine* says that it could have various senses, referring to resurrection or anointing to the office of mediator or exaltation above the angels on being anointed king.[1] In both the passages just quoted the Son's exaltation above the angels is mentioned, but in the third book his anointing to the office of mediator is also important, as appears in the Argument: "The Son of God freely offers himself a Ransome for Man: the Father accepts him, ordains his incarnation, pronounces his exaltation above all Names in Heaven and Earth; commands all the Angels to adore him." Is it possible that this additional idea appeared to Milton to justify the repetition in a different setting? Or is it more likely that such duplication as there is resulted from the late composition of Book III? Milton wished to make that book a complete theological picture, and did not pause to consider whether other parts of the poem, either preceding or succeeding, presented the same facts in similar fashion.

Since in the plot of *Paradise Lost* the exaltation of the Son supplies the motive for Satan's rebellion, it is astonishing that in Books I and II "we hear nothing of Christ's exaltation, and Satan's hatred of the Son."[2] On the contrary, it is the Most High that Satan trusted to have equalled, and the Omnipotent who has foiled him. Nor is this true of references to Satan's rebellion in these books alone, but in the entire poem, except the story of the War in Heaven. In one instance Satan's jealousy is perhaps actually excluded: Adam in his despair concludes that he is

> To *Satan* only like both crime and doom.   (X. 841)

---

1. *Christian Doctrine*, 1.5 (Columbia ed., XIV, 180 ff.). See also Gilbert, "The Theological Basis of Satan's Rebellion" etc., *Modern Philology*, XL (1942), 23-26; and Arnold Williams, "The Motiva-

tion of Satan's Rebellion in *Paradise Lost*," *Studies in Philology*, XLII (1945), 253-67.
2. McColley, *Paradise Lost*, p. 99. The Son is mentioned only in II. 678.

This seems to refer to Satan as disobedient through pride in general rather than as protesting against the exaltation of Messiah.[3]

In Book VI itself the Son is forgotten when the reason given by the Grand Foe for his rebellion is that he and his followers

can allow

Omnipotence to none.   (VI. 158-59)

Abdiel, who when he defied Satan showed himself expert in theology, says nothing of Messiah in Book VI. Indeed the Son but once appears in that book before the Father sends him to overthrow the rebellious hosts; this one reference is indeed clear, for the Father says that the rebels refuse "for thir King Messiah" (VI. 42). The total effect, however, of this book is that Messiah, introduced in the Almighty's early speech and at last entrusted with the decision of the battle, was not originally so prominent. The speeches of Abdiel, perhaps written earlier than those in the preceding book, may have been originally assigned to some other angel, before the kingship of the Son was made crucial, and when Milton was still using only such reasons for angelic revolt as are given by Spenser:

3. Cf. also:

> Say Goddess, what ensu'd when *Raphael*,
> The affable Arch-Angel, had forewarn'd
> *Adam* by dire example to beware
> Apostasie, by what befell in Heaven
> To those Apostates, least the like befall
> In Paradise to *Adam* or his Race.
> (VII. 40-45)

Here, as in other references to Satan as apostate, nothing more than rebellion against God, without suggestion of the Son, need be found. John Calvin speaks of Adam's sin as "apostasia, qua se homo conditoris sui imperio subducit, imo eum reiicit et abnegat" (*Comm. in Genesin*, 3:6, col. 61—*Opera*, Brunsvigae, 1882, Vol. XXIII).

In *Paradise Lost* as it stands, pride is the cause of Satan's fall, as Milton announces in I. 36, as the Rebel himself says in IV. 40, and as Milton puts it in V. 665, saying that Satan through pride could not bear to see Messiah proclaimed king. In the last instance Satan is the more inclined to put pride into act because he is "fraught With envie against the Son of God" (V. 662; cf. VI. 793). Envy of man first appears in I. 35 and often thereafter (cf. Sec. 40, below). Satan's ambition is also mentioned as a cause of his fall (e.g., I. 41, IV. 40, 61). Pride or ambition then, once said by Milton to be backed with envy of the Son, is the cause of Lucifer's revolt.

> Pride impatient of long resting peace,
> Did puffe them up with greedy bold ambition,
> That they gan cast their state how to increase,
> Above the fortune of their first condition,
> And sit in Gods owne seat without commission.
>
> (*Hymne of Heavenly Love*, 78-82)

Calvin was willing to be still vaguer:

Many perhaps do grudge, that the Scripture doth not orderly and distinctly in many places set forth that fall and the cause, manner, time, and fashion thereof. . . . Let us be content shortly to know thus much concerning the nature of devils, that at the first creation they were the Angels of God: but by swarving out of kinde they both destroyed themselves and are become instrumentes of destruction to other."

(*Institutes* 1.14.16, trans. Norton, London, 1578)

A more specific cause is found in various authors earlier than Milton, though frequently linked with the Incarnation;[4] the latter may even take the first place; for example, Marino has Satan say:

> Volse a le forme sue semplici, e prime
> Natura sovra alzar corporea, e bassa,
> E de' membri del Ciel capo sublime
> Far di limo terrestre indegna massa.
> I no'l soffersi, e d'Aquilon le cime
> Salsi, ove d'Angel mai volo non passa.
>
> (*Strage degli Innocenti* 1.28)

It appears in the *Christian Doctrine* that Milton was willing to think of Christ as king of the angels without reference to the Incarnation.[5] This doctrine he may have taken from John Calvin.[6] The same opinion appears in the sixth book, although, as has been indicated, in the third the Exaltation and the Incarnation go together. Holding the theory that man was made to supply the place of the fallen angels, Milton would hardly, in the interests of his plot, have wished the Incarnation to be announced in Heaven before the angels fell,[7] but might have been willing to take the opinion of Calvin:

4. McColley, *op. cit.*, pp. 25-33.
5. *Doctrina Christiana*, 1.5 (Columbia ed., pp. 180 ff.).
6. *Institutes*, 2.12.7 (trans. Norton, London, 1578). Cf. *P.L.* VI. 886.

7. Vondel, in his *Lucifer*, by placing the fall of the angels after the creation of man, easily uses their jealousy of man and even of the prophesied Incarnation.

Finxerunt curiosi sophistae, quia [Satan] praeviderat filium Dei humana carne induendum, invidia simul flagrasse: verum frivola est speculatio. Nam quum homo factus sit Dei filius, ut nos ex misera dissipatione iam perditos colligeret, quomodo praevideri potuit quod futurum non erat nisi homo peccasset? Si coniecturis detur locus, verisimilius est (ut desperati solent) rabie quadam fuisse adactum, ut secum in societatem aeterni interitus hominem raperet. Verum hac una ratione contentos esse nos decet quod, quum esset Dei adversarius, conatus sit ordinem ab eo positum evertere: quia Deum non poterat e solio suo detrahere, hominem aggressus est, in quo refulgebat eius imago (*Commentarius in Genesin* 3.2—*Opera*, Brunsvigae, 1882, Vol. XXIII, col. 56)

In other parts of the poem, however, there are some indications that Satan felt wronged because he thought God intended to set man above the angels. Yet since Calvin had said that it was fond trifling to say that "the Angels were then set behinde menne,"[8] and Milton himself did not hold that belief,[9] the interpretation is wholly Lucifer's when he says that after making man, God

> Him Lord pronounc'd, and, O indignitie!
> Subjected to his service Angel wings,
> And flaming Ministers to watch and tend
> Thir earthy Charge;[10]   (IX. 154-57)

and further calls him

> this new Favorite
> Of Heav'n, this Man of Clay, Son of despite,
> Whom us the more to spite his Maker rais'd
> From dust.   (IX. 175-78)

It appears, then, that in the beginning Milton may have given to Satan's rebellion only the vague motives that satisfied Calvin and

8. *Institutes*, 2.12.6.
9. *Christian Doctrine*, 1.7 (Columbia ed., XV, 34-36); 1.9 (XV, 96-106); *Paradise Lost*, v. 490. In the last, man is apparently inferior in degree, though not in kind. Cf. VII. 157. Beelzebub reports man as less excellent than the angels but more favored by God (II. 350).
10. This is a perversion of "Minis-

terium eorum praecipuum circa fideles est. Heb. 1:14. omnes sunt spiritus ministrantes qui emittuntur ministerii causa propter heredes salutis" (*Christ. Doct.*, 1.9 [XV, 100]). Satan had earlier called this ministering slavery, though not to man, and Abdiel had refuted him (*P.L.* VI. 167, 182).

Spenser. He then felt that what Calvin calls "vain histories" of Satan
were suitable for his poem, being more concrete. Moreover the cause
chosen enabled him to give prominence to the Son—an advantage in a
plan that excluded man from the happiness symbolized by Eden only

> till one greater Man
> Restore us, and regain the blissful Seat.   (I. 4-5)

Doubtless Milton knew that anger over the Incarnation was often
associated with Satan's revolt against the kingship of Messiah.[11] This,
if the poet ever used it, was rejected, to appear only in Satan's general
objections against the dignity given to man.

If Milton had from the beginning of his epic plan attributed Satan's
rebellion to jealousy of Messiah, he could hardly have escaped some
incidental references to it. Its limitation to Books V and VI suggests
that it was determined on late, after Books I and II and most other
parts of the epic were written. Even the speakers in the Council of
Book II make no mention of the Son as their adversary, but only of
"Heav'ns all-ruling Sire." Deciding to give Satan the specific motive
of jealousy, Milton rewrote Books V and VI, leaving other parts of
his work essentially unchanged. When altering the account of Satan's
rebellion to admit the new matter, he also added Abdiel to present the
case against the Adversary,[12] and substituted for a victory by the faithful angels one by Messiah.[13]

11. Perhaps it is fanciful to find
    something of this in Satan's un-
    willingness to "incarnate" (IX.
    166) his would-be divine essence
    in the serpent.
12. See Sec. 37, below.
13. It is impossible to think of Mil-
    ton's fifth and sixth books with-
    out Revelation 12, where it is
    said that Michael and his angels
    fought with Satan and his host.
    It must not be assumed, how-
    ever, that Milton is following
    that chapter. In a reference to
    it he speaks of "the Dragon, put
    to second rout" (IV. 3); seem-
    ingly he followed the theologians
    who held that Revelation did not
refer to Satan's original expulsion from Heaven. For example,
Milton's favorite commentator
on Revelation, David Paraeus,
writes of the War in Heaven of
verse seven:

> Quid praelium hoc sibi velit:
> quando sit factum, explicare
> haud facile est.
> Sunt qui referant ad primum
> Diaboli lapsum, quando cum
> angelis suis Lucifer coelo detur-
> batus fuit.
> Id recte repudiat Ribera.—
> *Opera* (Francofurti, 1647).

Milton also makes clear that the
activity of Satan in *Paradise·Lost*

36. Satan Pursued through Chaos
(II. 996-98; III. 390-98; VI. 44-55, 710-16, 880-84)

SATAN, lying on the burning lake, takes comfort that

> the angry Victor hath recall'd
> His Ministers of vengeance and pursuit
> Back to the Gates of Heav'n.   (I. 169-71)

Later he alludes to the Almighty's "swift pursuers from Heav'n Gates"
(I. 326). Moloc asks:

> Who but felt of late
> When the fierce Foe hung on our brok'n Rear
> Insulting, and pursu'd us through the Deep,
> With what compulsion and laborious flight
> We sunk thus low?   (II. 77-81)

Belial also speaks of himself and his friends as "pursu'd" (II. 165).
The devils do not specifically fear the Son, for after the speech of
Mammon, Milton comments:

> so much the fear
> Of thunder and the Sword of Michael
> Wrought still within them.[1]   (II. 293-95)

Chaos also saw that

> Heav'n Gates
> Pourd out by millions her victorious Bands
> Pursuing.   (II. 996-98)

The Almighty's command, however, had not required his servants
to go so far:

> Go Michael of Celestial Armies Prince,
> And thou in Military prowess next

[1]. At their overthrow in Heaven the is not that of Revelation 12:10 by writing that

Satan, now first inflam'd with
    rage, came down,
The Tempter ere th' Accuser of
    man-kind.   (IV. 9-10)

Son came against them "grasping ten thousand Thunders" and "check'd His thunder in mid Volie" (VI. 836, 854; *Paradise Regained*, I. 90), yet thunder is more specifically the weapon of the Father (I. 93, 258; III. 393; V. 893; VI. 632, 713); in VII. 606 the thunders belong to both.

> Gabriel, lead forth to Battel these my Sons
> Invincible, lead forth my armed Saints
> By thousands and by millions rang'd for fight;
> Equal in number to that Godless crew
> Rebellious, them with Fire and hostile Arms
> Fearless assault, and to the brow of Heav'n
> Pursuing drive them out from God and bliss,
> Into thir place of punishment, the Gulf
> Of Tartarus, which ready opens wide
> His fiery Chaos to receave thir fall.   (VI. 44-55)

Apparently attack by the angels alone is still contemplated in the Argument of Book I, which reads: "Satan . . . was by the command of God driven out of Heaven with all his Crew into the great Deep." The text, however, speaks of Satan as hurled down by "the Almighty Power" ("the most High," "th'Omnipotent") (I. 40-49), rather than by secondary hands, and the Father says to the Son:

> Go then thou Mightiest in thy Fathers might,
> Ascend my Chariot, guide the rapid Wheeles
> That shake Heav'ns basis, bring forth all my Warr,
> My Bow and Thunder, my Almightie Arms
> Gird on, and Sword upon thy puissant Thigh;
> Pursue these sons of Darkness, drive them out
> From all Heav'ns bounds into the utter Deep.   (VI. 710-16)

But whether the Son's assuming of power given him by the Father is the carrying out of a command may be debated. At any rate the Father spoke after the faithful angels had proved unequal to the task, which then passed to the Son, who gave the order:

> Stand still in bright array ye Saints, here stand
> Ye Angels arm'd, this day from Battel rest;
>
> . . . .
>
> Number to this dayes work is not ordain'd
> Nor multitude, stand onely and behold
> Gods indignation on these Godless pourd
> By mee . . . .
> . . . . I alone against them.   (VI. 801-20)

And so it is done. Messiah drives the rebels before him; the wall of Heaven opens, and

> headlong themselves they threw
> Down from the verge of Heav'n, Eternal wrauth
> Burnt after them to the bottomless pit.   (VI. 864-66)

For nine days they fall, and at last Hell receives them.

> Sole Victor from th' expulsion of his Foes
> Messiah his triumphal Chariot turnd:
> To meet him all his Saints, who silent stood
> Eye witnesses of his Almightie Acts,
> With Jubilie advanc'd.   (VI. 880-84)

The word *expulsion* hints that Messiah did not pursue beyond the wall
of Heaven. Likewise in the angelic hymn after the Son undertakes the
Atonement:

> Hee . . . .
> . . . . by thee threw down
> Th' aspiring Dominations: thou that day
> Thy Fathers dreadful Thunder didst not spare,[2]
> Nor stop thy flaming Chariot wheels, that shook
> Heav'ns everlasting Frame, while o're the necks
> Thou drov'st of warring Angels disarraid.
> Back from pursuit thy Powers with loud acclaime
> Thee only extoll'd.   (III. 390-98)

Sin, in her account, seems to agree that the rebels merely fell, without
pursuit (II. 771). Raphael hardly implies pursuit outside Heaven when
he says that after Lucifer fell "through the deep into his place,"

> the great Son returnd
> Victorious with his Saints,   (VII. 135-36)

and that the Creator, Father and Son, or Jehovah, is greater in Creation
than in his return "from the Giant Angels" (VII. 605). Some accounts,
then, speak of Satan and his legions as pursued by Michael and his

2. Does *didst not spare* mean *did not use sparingly* or merely *did not fail to use?* In the detailed account we read that he "check'd His Thunder in mid Volie" (VI. 853-54). In the hymn after the Creation the angels sing: "Thee that day Thy Thunders magnifi'd" (VII. 605-6); but in the detailed account he used "ten thousand Thunders" (VI. 836)—quite enough to magnify the user, and wholly adequate.

hosts, while others, including the most detailed, give the victory to
Messiah and do not assert pursuit beyond the wall of Heaven.

Of the two forms, that of victory by the Son is evidently the later,
since it now forms the main narrative, while the victory and pursuit
by angels is mentioned only incidentally. Such angelic pursuit is evidently part of the story as planned when Michael and the angels rather
than Messiah were conquerors in Heaven. When Milton, changing
the outcome of the celestial struggle, modified parts of the fifth and
sixth books, allusions elsewhere in the epic were left unchanged.

Certain words spoken by Sin appear to belong to the latest plan:

> Warr arose,
> And fields were fought in Heav'n; wherein remaind
> (For what could else) to our Almighty Foe
> Cleer Victory, to our part loss and rout
> Through all the Empyrean: down they fell
> Driv'n headlong from the Pitch of Heaven, down
> Into this Deep, and in the general fall
> I also.   (II. 767-74)

She mentions neither angelic victory nor pursuit beyond the "Pitch
of Heaven." This passage, then, is probably later than the appearance
of Messiah on the third day of battle.[3] Likewise early lines in Book I
do not make the angels assist "the Almighty Power" in hurling Satan
"headlong flaming from th' Ethereal Skie" (line 45). Evidently this
too is later than the Messianic defeat of Lucifer. It has, however, been
suggested that at one time the War in Heaven began in the second
paragraph of the first book of *Paradise Lost*,[4] and that lines 40-49 were
substituted when the long account was transferred. This would mean
that Milton had decided to take the victory from the hands of Michael
before he shifted the defeat of Satan. However it is also possible that
lines 40-49—so prominent by position that they would not be left
out of harmony with the main narrative—originally spoke of Michael
and his hosts as conquerors and were later changed to their present
form.

3. For the late date of the story of   4. Sec. 18, above.
   Sin and Death, see Sec. 38, below.

37. Abdiel
(v. 804-907; vi. 14-43, 99-202)

SATAN, having drawn his host to the regions of the North, addresses
to them a bold speech attacking the Father and the Son. Suddenly
there rises a speaker hitherto unknown in the poem, Abdiel, the servant
of God,[1]

> then whom none with more zeale ador'd
> The Deitie, and divine commands obei'd.   (v. 805-6)

His speech is a defence of the "just decree of God" by which the Son,
the creating Word of the Almighty, is set up as rightful king. Satan
answers haughtily, declaring that the angels were "self-begot" at the
time set by "fatal course" (v. 861). He concludes with a threat, to
which Abdiel boldly answers with a prediction of divine punishment.
Abdiel here speaks as a bold theologian, using scriptural language to
refute the unsound reasoning of Satan. Much of what he says might
have been derived from Milton's own *Christian Doctrine* and various
other of his writings, so that the seraph may be called the poet's
mouthpiece.[2] In character too, Abdiel is what Milton might have
wished himself to be, the one faithful among a faithless multitude,
unmoved by the example of the many, sustaining the truth without

1. Students of Milton ignorant of Hebrew, like the present writer, have sought in vain for an angel named Abdiel and have even supposed that Milton devised him, applying to him a name found in the Bible (1 Chron., 5:15) and meaning *Servant of God*. The name, however, is traditionally that of an angel, being found in the *Book of Raziel* (Amsterdam, 1701, p. 4b) in a list of Seven Angels including Michael and Raphael; little information is given about him. *The Book of Raziel* perhaps dates back to the eighth century (Oesterley and Box, *A Short Survey of the Literature of Rabbinical and Mediaeval Judaism*, New York, 1920, p. 238), and Trithemius and Agrippa are indebted to it (M. Gaster, "The Sword of Moses," *The Journal of the Royal Asiatic Society*, ser. 3, 1896, p. 161). Directly or indirectly its mention of Abdiel may well have come under Milton's eye.

   I owe the reference to the *Book of Raziel* to Rabbi Samuel S. Cohon. Professor W. F. Stinespring translated for me the pertinent part of it and gave me other information.
2. This I present in detail in "The Theological Basis of Satan's Rebellion and the Function of Abdiel in *Paradise Lost*," *Modern Philology*, XL (1942), 20-39.

fear of their numbers. This is stated when the undaunted seraph is commended by the Father:

> Servant of God, well done, well hast thou fought
> The better fight, who single hast maintaind
> Against revolted multitudes the Cause
> Of Truth, in word mightier then they in Armes;
> And for the testimonie of Truth hast born
> Universal reproach, far worse to beare
> Then violence: for this was all thy care
> To stand approv'd in sight of God, though Worlds
> Judg'd thee perverse.   (VI. 29-37)

After this assertion of the truth of his words, Abdiel is addressed by the Father as though he were a leader of the celestial hosts:

> The easier conquest now
> Remains thee, aided by this host of friends,
> Back on thy foes more glorious to return
> Then scornd thou didst depart, and to subdue
> By force, who reason for thir Law refuse,
> Right reason for thir Law, and for thir King
> Messiah, who by right of merit Reigns.

From commendation of the right reason of this dreadless angel, the Almighty turns abruptly to the normal leaders of the hosts of heaven, Michael and Gabriel, instructing them to go forth to battle. They meet the host of Satan and

> the shout
> Of Battle now began, and rushing sound
> Of onset ended soon each milder thought.   (VI. 96-98)

This says that the combat begins, but actually it does not, for in the narrow space between the hosts Satan appears

> before the cloudie Van,
> On the rough edge of battel ere it joyn'd.

Abdiel, seeing him, decides within his heart that having won "in debate of Truth" he should also win in arms. He steps forward to defy Satan, concluding:

> Now learn too late
> How few somtimes may know, when thousands err.
>
> (VI. 147-48)

Satan answers insultingly, comparing Abdiel's servility with his own
freedom. This leads Abdiel to a Miltonic discourse on freedom:

> This is servitude,
> To serve th' unwise, or him who hath rebelld
> Against his worthier, as thine now serve thee,
> Thy self not free, but to thy self enthrall'd.

Concluding, he strikes Satan's helm with a blow that drives the rebel
to his knee.

> Amazement seis'd
> The Rebel Thrones, but greater rage to see
> Thus foil'd thir mightiest. (VI. 198-200)

Then comes the long delayed onset:

> Now storming furie rose,
> And clamour such as heard in Heav'n till now
> Was never, Arms on Armour clashing bray'd
> Horrible discord.

It appears, then, that Milton says that the general combat has begun,
but really delays it for more than a hundred lines to give Abdiel opportunity for a striking exploit.

As the struggle continues,

> Satan, who that day
> Prodigious power had shewn, and met in Armes
> No equal, (VI. 246-48)

at last, encountering Michael, is wounded and defeated, so that his
followers carry him out of danger. He lies

> Gnashing for anguish and despite and shame
> To find himself not matchless, and his pride
> Humbl'd by such rebuke, so farr beneath
> His confidence to equal God in power. (VI. 340-43)

Both these statements by Milton disregard the encounter in which he
was "foil'd" (line 200) by Abdiel. Evidently they come from a state

of the poem in which Satan did not fight that combat. Since in continuous composition the poet could hardly have written two incidents
in both of which Satan is represented as first meeting his match, the
episode of the "dauntless angel" is evidently an interpolation. The
peculiarities noted in the earlier part of Book VI fit such a suggestion.
Moreover, Abdiel is not mentioned along with Michael and Gabriel
in the Argument of Book VI. In the course of the battle he overthrew
Ariel, Arioc, and Ramiel (vi. 369-72). As a fairly important angel, he
might have been named for these exploits before he was chosen to encounter Satan.

It need not be supposed that the story of Abdiel in the two books
formed an original unit. In Book V his interest is theological, in VI it
is political.[3] His early activity has no effect on the plot, since he neither
restrains Lucifer nor brings warning to the all-knowing God; indeed
on approaching the throne he

found

> Already known what he for news had thought
> To have reported.   (vi. 19-21)

His function in Book V relates to the ideas of the poem. Having made
jealousy of the Son the cause of Satan's rebellion, Milton wished as it
were to anticipate such later readers as Shelley. In the Preface to
Prometheus Unbound that admirer of the "sacred Milton" recognized
that Satan's character was tainted with "ambition, envy, revenge, and
a desire for personal aggrandizement," yet held that his wrongs "ex-
ceed all measure." Abdiel's speeches are Milton's attempts to make
clear to his reader that Satan has suffered no wrongs that might excuse
his desire to sit on the throne of Heaven. The scene in the assembly
of the rebels shows at its best Milton's capacity to unite idea and dramatic action. Evidently it was composed after the decision to make
jealousy of Messiah the cause of Satan's revolt. Having an important
place in Book V, "the fervent angel" deserved further attention. So
Milton devised and interpolated Abdiel's part in Book VI, to emphasize the truth of his theology as well as to balance with physical power
his earlier mental vigor:

3. See pp. 34-39 of the article cited in note 2.

His puissance . . . .
I mean to try, whose Reason I have tri'd
Unsound and false; nor is it aught but just,
That he who in debate of Truth hath won,
Should win in Arms, in both disputes alike
Victor. (VI. 119-24)

38. Sin and Death
(II. 648-883, 1023-32; X. 230-409)

UNLIKE ALL Milton's other plans for dramas, those for *Paradise Lost*
and *Adam unparadiz'd* call for allegorical characters. The list in-
creases from plan to plan, until in the third it includes twenty-four.
In the fourth the number is reduced; the only ones mentioned are
Mercy, Faith, Hope, and Charity, though the "mask of all the evills
of this life" presumably includes the fifteen "mutes" of Plan Three.

Except for Sin and Death, *Paradise Lost* does not contain many
allegorical names, though there are some; for example, War has a
brazen throat (XI. 713); Love has golden shafts (IV. 763); Wisdom is
the sister of the Holy Spirit (VII. 9); Despair tends the sick (XI. 490);
Misery is Death's harbinger (IX. 13); but none of these are elaborated
as the tragic plans would lead us to expect. One detail, however, seems
to have been carried over: the use of the word *shape*. In the fourth
plan "conscience in a shape accuses him," and the angel "causes to pass
before his eyes in Shapes a mask of all the evills of this life & world."
In the epic, the word is used of Sin and Death:

Before the Gates there sat
On either side a formidable shape; . . . .
. . . . . The other shape,
If shape it might be call'd that shape had none, (II. 648-67)

and Satan addresses Death as "execrable shape" (II. 681). These two
instances in *Paradise Lost* might be put under the common meaning,
frequent in the poem, but seem to have a flavor of that in the dramatic
plan.

Though so important in the epic, Death is but one of the mutes in
Plan Three and probably in Four. Sin is unmentioned in the drafts.
Milton then had in his dramatic plans the general idea of allegory but

no specific suggestions for the allegorical passages of *Paradise Lost*. In fact, Sin and Death are found in parts of the poem far removed from drama. They first appear in Hell, in a setting wholly epic, and their great action is the building of the bridge over Chaos. Death in such activity is quite different from him who shook his dart over the sick in the lazar-house, but delayed to strike (XI. 492). Sin and Death are, then, late comers in Milton's work in so far as he could not have had them in mind until he decided on an epic with a theme allowing them parts.[1]

It seems that their appearance in the tenth book was devised later than that in the second. Their building of the bridge over Chaos is told briefly in Book II (1023-34) and at length in X (282-323, 350-82). Why did Milton give the second account as something new, without making any reference to his earlier verses? Or why, if he was to elaborate the building of the bridge, did he not drop the earlier account? The following show the likeness between the two:

following his track	(II. 1025)
according to the track that Satan first made;	(X. Arg.)
following the track Of Satan;	(X. 314-15)
a broad and beat'n way	(II. 1026)
broad as the Gate	(X. 298)
a passage broad, Smooth, easie, inoffensive down to Hell.	(X. 304-5)
As with a Trident smote, and fix't as firm	(X. 295)
to make the way easier . . . they pave a broad Highway;	(X. Arg.)
Over the dark Abyss	(II. 1027)
Over the vext Abyss;	(X. 314)

1. Dr. Johnson perhaps had in mind that they are not necessary to the plot when he wrote: "To this [allegory] there was no tempta- tion, but the author's opinion of its beauty" ("Milton," par. 258, in *Lives of the English Poets* [Oxford, 1905], I. 186).

whose boiling Gulf	(II. 1027)
over this Gulfe	(X. 253)
foaming deep;	(X. 301)
a Bridge of wondrous length	(II. 1028)

a Bridge

Of length prodigious;	(X. 301-2)

reaching th' utmost Orbe

Of this frail World;	(II. 1029-30)

joyning to the Wall

Immovable of this now fenceless world;	(X. 302-3)
With easie intercourse pass to and fro	(II. 1031)
easie	(X. 305)
from Hell to this World to and fro;	(X. Arg.)
Pav'd after him	(II. 1026)
they pave a broad Highway.	(X. Arg.)

There is one contrast in the response of Chaos itself:

whose boiling Gulf

Tamely endur'd a Bridge of wondrous length	(II. 1027-28)

Disparted *Chaos* over built exclaimd, And with rebounding surge the barrs assaild, That scorn'd his indignation.	(X. 416-18)

Curiously, the Argument of the tenth book is in some words nearer to the account in Book II than to that in X. It is apparent that the two narratives tend toward the identical; at least they are not planned to supplement each other.

In the tenth book, Sin and Death provide a road for Satan down to Hell, but that road is not indispensable; if he had gone up through the Abyss without a bridge, he could go down through it without one. If the two allegorical figures had not been put into this book we should not demand them. Moreover, in Book II the bridge has been described as though in full, and its makers seem dismissed. Coming to the tenth book, Milton saw an opportunity to give a striking end to the work of Satan who, by going to Hell, abandons for the time his activity in the world. In the dramatic plans Lucifer disappears, save for a reference to his example, inserted as an afterthought in Plan Four, but Sin and Death become his representatives in the epic, though they are to fulfil the Father's will by licking up

> the draff and filth
> Which mans polluting Sin with taint hath shed
> On what was pure.   (x. 630-32)

Moreover at last they will be sealed up in Hell. By this example Milton again affirms that evil can never conquer; God's ways can be justified even by means of Sin and Death. To bring them again into action, the account of the bridge was expanded and put in the tenth book.

It is difficult to see any reason for the repetition of an incident in both a brief and an expanded form, with no apparent relation between them. Milton repeats words and ideas with apparent purpose, but the repetition of an allegorical action seems to be a different thing. If Milton had the entire manuscript read straight through to him after it was completed, he would have been likely to have caught such an obvious repetition, if unintentional. We do not, however, know that he did have the poem so read. Then there is always the difficulty of a blind man in revision. If this repetition is intentional, the artistic reasons for it should be apparent; yet it is difficult to find them in this summary of an action later to be described in full.

39. Hell in Book X
(x. 413-584)

IN MILTON's dramatic plans there is no suggestion that Satan is to appear surrounded with followers; he is always solitary. Hence much of the part of Book X concerned with him can hardly have been written until Milton settled on the epic form. By passing from the return of the Son, after the judgment of Adam and Eve (x. 228), to the sending of the angels to bring on Adam extremes of heat and cold (x. 649), one can omit Satan without feeling a gap.

Though the activity in Hell in this book does not contribute to movement of the plot, it has its structural function. The importance of the Devil and of the doings in the lower world early in the epic demands something to balance it in the latter part. Otherwise these powerful early scenes recede into the past and the end of *Paradise Lost* seems so different from the beginning as to have little to do with it. Satan's return to Hell not merely supplies a counterpoise, but also brings back to the reader the memory of the early books and encourages him to fuse their effect with that of the final ones. Without Satan in Hell, the block of material derived from the early tragedy extends from the beginning of Book IX to the end—a human drama somewhat varied by short scenes in Heaven. By the Devil's return to Pandaemonium, that block is split in two, to secure the variety Milton so cherished.

Moreover, Milton does not care to leave his reader with the feeling that Satan has succeeded, or even that he can escape with impunity. He wishes to remind us that the Devil of the earlier books, for all the vaunting that has deceived and shall deceive so many readers, has only "semblance of worth, not substance"; the comic futility in which we last see him asserts that the power of God is irresistible even in the center of the empire in which the Adversary pretends to glory.

The scene can hardly have been composed as early as Books I and II; at least it comes from a time when the poet viewed his work as a unit and had estimated its effect part by part and as a whole. But though presumably late, this passage still seems to incorporate something from the third draft in the Cambridge Manuscript, namely Lucifer's "insulting in what he had don to the destruction of man":

> A World who would not purchase with a bruise,
> Or much more grievous pain?   (x. 500-1)

Milton kept his early material in mind until the end.

40. Satan's Foreknowledge of Man's Creation
(I. 650-54; II. 345-53, 830-35; VII. 150-59; IX. 135-42)

WHEN LUCIFER first assembles his followers in Hell, he suggests to them that their enmity may express itself on God's new creation,

> whereof so rife
> There went a fame in Heav'n that he ere long

> Intended to create, and therein plant
> A generation, whom his choice regard
> Should favour equal to the Sons of Heaven.   (I. 650-54)

Beelzebub, without allusion to these words, later repeats their sense, adding that God confirmed his purpose with an oath:

> There is a place
> (If ancient and prophetic fame in Heav'n
> Err not) another World, the happy seat
> Of some new Race call'd *Man*, about this time
> To be created like to us, though less
> In power and excellence, but favour'd more
> Of him who rules above; so was his will
> Pronounc'd among the Gods, and by an Oath,
> That shook Heav'ns whol circumference, confirm'd.
> > (II. 345-53)

Satan sets out to find this new world, if possible, though to Sin and Death he does not profess certainty of its existence (II. 837-39). He is glad to be informed by Chaos that his sea is to find a shore (II. 1011), that is, that the world is near. Perhaps he even gains confidence that the rumor of its creation is well founded, for though Chaos does not mention man, Satan by the time he reaches Uriel does not doubt the existence of this new creature, for he asks to see

> chiefly Man,
> His chief delight and favour, him for whom
> All these his works so wondrous he ordaind.   (III. 663-65)

When Satan later shows his knowledge of the Creation, he is precise about the Six Days, which he has had no means for learning, but uncertain about the length of the Creator's preparation:

> To mee shall be the glorie sole among
> The infernal Powers, in one day to have marr'd
> What he *Almightie* styl'd, six Nights and Days
> Continu'd making, and who knows how long
> Before had bin contriving, though perhaps
> Not longer then since I in one Night freed
> From servitude inglorious welnigh half
> Th' Angelic Name.   (IX. 135-42)

This precludes the "fame" of which Satan earlier spoke, and still more the oath mentioned by Beelzebub, since it implies that no one knew of the plan for creating man until angelic rebellion made it necessary; indeed the Adversary hints that before the revolt God would have had no possibility of planning for Man to take the room left by the fallen angels.

Except in the first two books, the purpose of the creation of man is usually to provide a substitute for the angels expelled, whether the speaker is Satan (III. 678; IV. 359; IX. 148) or the Almighty himself, who explains it most fully:

> Least his heart exalt him in the harme
> Already done, to have dispeopl'd Heav'n
> My damage fondly deem'd, I can repaire
> That detriment, if such it be to lose
> Self-lost, and in a moment will create
> Another World, out of one man a Race
> Of men innumerable, there to dwell,
> Not here, till by degrees of merit rais'd
> They open to themselves at length the way
> Up hither.   (VII. 150-59)

This passage perhaps gives some support to Satan's guess that the creation of man was not determined upon until after the War in Heaven; at least it does not say that God in his foreknowledge arranged to supply the place of the devils before they rebelled.

With one exception, the prophecies of man given in the first and second books do not represent him as formed to fill the spaces left empty in Heaven,[1] but merely say that he is favored as much as or more than the angels. Such different treatment of the theme is in part structural. If, as in Books I and II, Satan is to go out against man, he must know of man's existence. This he must either have learned before he left Heaven or afterward. Milton commonly uses the first plan. Flat contradiction is found only between Satan's knowledge of

---

1. This "ancient prophesie," report, or tradition appears in the Arguments of Books I and II.

Dr. Johnson noticed that Milton does not invariably assume it, writing: "The creation of man is represented as the consequence of the vacuity left in heaven by the expulsion of the rebels; yet Satan mentions it as 'rife in heaven' before his departure" ("Milton," par. 259, *op. cit.*, I. 186).

a rumor and his ignorance of the time when the formation of man was decided on. Such ignorance appears in a passage in which Lucifer in the Garden is bemoaning himself and seeking revenge on man already created, according to the fourth draft in the Cambridge Manuscript. Books I and II, on the other hand, in which Satan is not ignorant, are epic material, relating to a time when Satan had not seen the world and man. The contradiction doubtless is to be explained by the length of time between the composition of the two passages.

In the second book the themes of man as a substitute for the fallen angels and of the prophecy of the World's creation are once combined. Satan's knowledge is asserted, though without giving its basis; he speaks to Sin and Death of

> a place foretold
> Should be, and, by concurring signs, ere now
> Created vast and round, a place of bliss
> In the Pourlieues of Heav'n, and therein plac't
> A race of upstart Creatures, to supply
> Perhaps our vacant room;   (II. 830-35)

there is a similar passage in a later conversation with Sin and Death (x. 481-85). It has been shown that Satan's ignorance of God's plan appears only in the ninth book and that man as a supplanter is normal except in the first two books. If, as has been suggested,[2] the story of Sin and Death is late, it is probable that when Milton came to write it he would use the ideas most common in the poem, in spite of the improbability that the rumor of Creation would have been spread in Heaven before the rebellion that left space for new inhabitants.

When Satan says that he knows not when man's creation was planned, that he guesses, indeed, that it was not until after his own fall, Milton might be following the notion that the rebel angels were expelled before man was made. When Satan knows of "fame" in Heaven that man was to be created, he has the knowledge that makes Milton's plot easiest. But when Beelzebub asserts that the Almighty confirmed by oath that man should be created like angels, less powerful, "but favour'd more Of him who rules above" (II. 350-51), a third possibility is hinted. The situation is somewhat like that in Vondel's *Lucifer*, in which the Almighty orders a solemn proclamation telling of the Crea-

2. See Sec. 38, above.

tion of Man and his union with Messiah so that the seed of Adam shall sit higher than the angels. Possibly Milton's plans went through three stages, of which the first was simple revolt because of Satan's desire to sit higher than God. Wishing to give a more evident motive, Milton, after considering the tradition, may have planned to give Satan the motive of objection to the Incarnation; at that time were written the words just quoted from Beelzebub. But this scheme did not fit with the poet's Christology, which made the Son the obvious creator, or with the opinion expressed in the *Christian Doctrine* that it is "verisimilius" that the angels fell before the universe came into being.[3] So Milton changed to the present form of the story, leaving Beelzebub's words to hint at the processes he went through before reaching satisfaction.[4]

3. See I. 7, 9 (Columbia ed., pp. 34, 96).

4. The present council and the anointing of the Son as the cause of rebellion are both probably of late composition (Sec. 50, Group VI, below). It is not unlikely, however, that Beelzebub's speech, related to Satan's (I. 650-54), was taken over into the present council when the earlier one was abandoned (see Secs. 3 and 31, above).

CHAPTER SEVEN

MISCELLANEOUS INCONSISTENCIES AND INSERTIONS

41. The Last Things
(III. 326-38; X. 636-37; XII. 458-64, 546-49)

FIVE times Milton mentions the end of the world, as set forth in Revelation 20 and 21, and II Peter. In the angelic hymn after Messiah agrees to bear man's sins, there appear the Last Judgment, the closing of Hell, and the new Heaven and new Earth (III. 326-38). The Almighty, looking on the seemingly victorious Sin and Death, prophesies that they shall be

> Through *Chaos* hurld, obstruct the mouth of Hell
> For ever, and seal up his ravenous Jawes.   (x. 636-37)

The new Heaven and the new Earth are prophesied by Michael, at the end of Adam's vision of the Flood (XI. 900). The Last Judgment is further foretold by Michael as a conclusion to the life of Messiah, who

> shall come,
> When this worlds disolution shall be ripe,
> With glory and power to judge both quick and dead,
> To judge th' unfaithful dead, but to reward
> His faithful, and receave them into bliss,
> Whether in Heav'n or Earth, for then the Earth
> Shall all be Paradise.   (XII. 458-64)

Again the Savior shall return

> to dissolve
> *Satan* with his perverted World, then raise

> From the conflagrant mass, purg'd and refin'd,
> New Heav'ns, new Earth. (XII. 546-49)

It has been explained that the third book as a summary of Christian doctrine is likely to repeat any important matter of faith given in other parts of the epic.[1] It is less clear why in the twelfth book Milton should twice draw on II Peter 2: "All these things shall be dissolved," in passages little more than a hundred lines apart. Each of the passages concludes a section of the poem. The first is of some hundred and fifty lines on the work of Messiah, to which his part in the Last Judgment forms a fitting close. Having finished the exposition of this, the angel pauses "as at the Worlds great period" (XII. 467) and Adam, after expressing his wonder, asks what will betide the saints during the absence of the Deliverer. The angel then sets forth the persecutions of the Church, ending again with the overthrow of the perverted world and the foundation of the new one at the Last Judgment. It is evident that each section is artistically concluded with the Dissolution, and moreover that the two sections are involved with each other. If Milton had decided to eliminate either reference to the end of the world, he must have revised the connected passages. If the first had been omitted he must have omitted also the angel's pause "at the Worlds great period," and Adam's exclamation:

> O goodness infinite, goodness immense!
> That all this good of evil shall produce,
> And evil turn to good. (XII. 469-71)

He could then have developed his second reference to the Last Things and combined Adam's omitted exclamation with his comment (XII. 553 ff.) on the angel's discourse on persecution. This would have required labor. Perhaps Milton, though seeing the repetition, felt that the two sections in themselves were so well handled that further re-writing would not be likely to produce total improvement.

It still seems unlikely, however, that two passages so similar are the result of consecutive composition. From the time of the fourth draft in the Cambridge Manuscript, Milton was intending to deal with the promise of the Messiah. Hence the survey of the life of Jesus may be taken as derived from that early plan. But the account of the per-

1. See Secs. 33 and 34, above.

secution of the Church, as the successor of the "mask of all the evills of this life & world," seemingly is of later planning. Hence its concluding reference to the Dissolution may well be later than that of the preceding passage in both plan and composition. When once the two were in verse, they satisfied Milton's standards.

42. The Punishment of Damned Men
(II. 596-614)

IN THE MIDST of the narrative of the occupations of the devils in Hell come the verses

> Thither by harpy-footed Furies hail'd,
> At certain revolutions all the damn'd
> Are brought. . . . .
> From Beds of raging Fire to starve in Ice
> Thir soft Ethereal warmth.   (II. 596-601)

Since Milton held that the place prepared for the Devil and his angels was the same as that for the punishment of wicked men,[1] what is being described is not what happened to Satan's followers but the state of damned human beings long after. The description continues to line 614, where it ends in the middle of the verse. Milton, it seems, might here have given warning that he was for the moment not dealing with the devils, as he does by the word *hereafter* in telling of the Limbo of Vanity (III. 444). The present passage seems like a fragment from a description of the punishments of men in Hell, possibly part of an early plan for this book.

There is an obvious difficulty in the word *ethereal*, which Milton uses elsewhere with the normal meaning of *heavenly* or at least of *relating to the ether*. Two passages in the *Aeneid* may be compared:

> Quem si fata virum servant, si vescitur aura
> Aetheria, neque adhuc crudelibus occubat umbris,
> Non metus.[2]   (I. 546-48)

1. *De Doctrina Christiana*, 1.33 (Columbia ed., p. 372).
2. Cf. Statius, *Thebaid*, 1.236-37:

nec iam amplius aethere nostro
Vescitur.

> Quam vellent aethere in alto
> Nunc et pauperiem et duros perferre labores! (vi. 436-37)

In each instance the world of men is compared with the lower world.[3]
It may be that Milton is suggesting the effect of Hell on the shade
from the earth, or possibly *ethereal* refers to the airiness of the shade,

> Par levibus ventis volucrique simillima somno.
>
> (*Aen.* vi. 702)

In any case this difficulty would seem not to overthrow the general
sense of the passage as relating to the damned of later times.

43. Satan's Freedom

(I. 209-15, 239-41; III. 80-84; X. 5-11, 616-32)

AT HIS first appearance Satan

>   lay
> Chain'd on the burning Lake, nor ever thence
> Had ris'n or heav'd his head, but that the will
> And high permission of all-ruling Heaven
> Left him at large to his own dark designs. (I. 209-13)

Yet soon Milton asserts that he and Beelzebub glory

>   to have scap't the Stygian flood
> As Gods, and by thir own recover'd strength,
> Not by the sufferance of supernal Power. (I. 239-41)

Satan, however, when wishing to make his exploring voyage appear
difficult, declares that

> Our prison strong, this huge convex of Fire,
> Outrageous to devour, immures us round
> Ninefold, and gates of burning Adamant
> Barr'd over us prohibit all egress. (II. 434-37)

And it seems that he could not have gone out if Sin had not opened the
gate for him. But later, in boasting to Gabriel, Satan implies that he
escaped by his own power:

3. The first applicable reference in *N.E.D.* is of 1697.

> let him surer barr
> His Iron Gates, if he intends our stay
> In that dark durance.   (iv. 897-99)

And perhaps the angel accepts this, for he answers that he will drag
his adversary back to the infernal pit

> And Seale thee so, as henceforth not to scorne
> The facil gates of hell too slightly barrd.   (iv. 966-67)

Even the Almighty speaks of Satan as "scap't" (v. 225), and says
formally:

> Onely begotten Son, seest thou what rage
> Transports our adversarie, whom no bounds
> Prescrib'd, no barrs of Hell, nor all the chains
> Heapt on him there, nor yet the main Abyss
> Wide interrupt can hold.   (iii. 80-84)

But to believe that Satan has power to escape against the will of God
is impossible to one holding Milton's view of divine omnipotence:

> For what can scape the Eye
> Of God All-seeing, or deceave his Heart
> Omniscient, who in all things wise and just,
> Hinder'd not Satan to attempt the minde
> Of Man?   (x. 5-9)

The truth of the matter is given in an incidental remark by Raphael
on his "excursion toward the Gates of Hell" to see that none of the
devils are spying on the work of Creation:

> Not that they durst without his leave attempt.   (viii. 237)

This takes us back to the first statement on Satan's rising from the
burning lake only through "Gods high sufferance for the tryal of man"
(i. 366); this is expressed later when the Almighty looks on Sin and
Death:

> See with what heat these Dogs of Hell advance
> To waste and havoc yonder World, which I
> So fair and good created, and had still
> Kept in that State, had not the folly of Man
> Let in these wastful Furies, who impute
> Folly to mee, so doth the Prince of Hell

> And his Adherents, that with so much ease
> I suffer them to enter and possess
> A place so heav'nly, and conniving seem
> To gratifie my scornful Enemies,
> That laugh, as if transported with some fit
> Of Passion, I to them had quitted all,
> At random yielded up to their misrule;
> And know not that I call'd and drew them thither
> My Hell-hounds, to lick up the draff and filth
> Which mans polluting Sin with taint hath shed
> On what was pure. (x. 616-32)

It seems unlikely that mere inadvertence or falling into an unCalvinistic notion of the power of Satan would have led Milton to allow the Almighty, in his formal speech in the third book, to imply that Satan could not be kept in Hell.[1] Rather, the poet is merely emphasizing Satan's activity. Indeed, it is of little import just how Satan gets out of Hell, for man himself, fully equipped to resist, is the cause of his own fall:

> So will fall,
> Hee and his faithless Progenie: whose fault?
> Whose but his own? ingrate, he had of mee
> All he could have; I made him just and right,
> Sufficient to have stood, though free to fall. (III. 95-99)

44. The Size of Satan's Host
(v. 710; VI. 49; IX. 141)

VARYING ACCOUNTS are given of the number of angels who rebelled. Raphael reports that Satan

> Drew after him the third part of Heav'ns Host. (v. 710)

1. After Satan's revolt begins the Father says to the Son:

> Let us advise, and to this hazard draw
> With speed what force is left, and all imploy
> In our defence, lest unawares we lose

> This our high place, our Sanctuarie, our Hill.
> (v. 729-32)

But this is obviously God's little joke (v. 718, 735-37) at the expense of Satan's folly in thinking to surprise omniscience. See *Christian Doctrine* I.9 (Col. ed., XV. 108).

Lucifer himself gives the same figure when he attempts to refute Abdiel (VI. 156), and it is that of Death (II. 692). In soliloquy Satan raises it to "welnigh half Th' Angelic Name" (IX. 141). The Almighty, when sending forth Gabriel and Michael to war, speaks of their numbers as "equal" to those of the rebels (VI. 49), and earlier he had said that he was to employ all his forces (V. 730); yet elsewhere he asserts that "far the greater part" have been faithful (VII. 145).

Seemingly Milton suited the number to the speaker and the circumstances.

45. The Days of Satan's Rebellion
(v. 682 - vi. 685)

IN THE NIGHT after the proclamation of the Son as the Begotten and Anointed, Satan did not sleep. He roused his second in command and told him that they were ordered to go to their possessions in the North "ere yet dim Night Her shadowie Cloud withdraws" (V. 685-86); his lieutenant repeated it in the form "ere dim Night had disincumberd Heav'n" (V. 700). Apparently Satan's host marched at once, and "at length" came "into the limits of the North" (V. 755). Satan addressed them, and Abdiel answered. Then,

> All night the dreadless Angel unpursu'd
> Through Heav'ns wide Champain held his way, till Morn,
> Wak't by the circling Hours, with rosie hand
> Unbarr'd the gates of Light.   (VI. 1-4)

Somewhat later the two armies met and the combat began, to continue without decision for

> Two dayes, as we compute the dayes of Heav'n.   (VI. 685)

On the third the Messiah expelled Satan and his host.

Elsewhere the rebellion is indicated as moving more slowly; in her narrative to Satan, Sin tells of her own birth

> at th' Assembly, and in sight
> Of all the Seraphim with thee combin'd
> In bold conspiracy against Heav'ns King.   (II. 749-51)

Admitting that she was at first held a sign portentous, she continues:

> familiar grown,
> I pleas'd, and with attractive graces won
> The most averse, thee chiefly, who full oft
> Thy self in me thy perfect image viewing
> Becam'st enamour'd, and such joy thou took'st
> With me in secret, that my womb conceiv'd
> A growing burden. Mean while Warr arose,
> And fields were fought in Heav'n.   (II. 761-68)

Satan's conspiracy here develops gradually, instead of arising and being carried out immediately after the proclamation of the Son. Even the War in Heaven is suggested as long, in harmony with the assertion that Satan's voice had been

> heard so oft
> In worst extreams, and on the perilous edge
> Of battel when it rag'd, in all assaults
> Thir surest signal.   (I. 275-78)

Something of the habitual is also apparent in the naming of Satan's Royal Seat, after he withdrew to the North:

> The Palace of great *Lucifer*, (so call
> That Structure in the Dialect of men
> Interpreted) which not long after, he
> Affecting all equality with God,
> In imitation of that Mount whereon
> *Messiah* was declar'd in sight of Heav'n,
> The Mountain of the Congregation call'd.   (V. 760-66)

On the other hand, the narrative of the War is supported by Satan's boast in soliloquy:

> I in one Night freed
> From servitude inglorious welnigh half
> Th' Angelic Name.   (IX. 140-42)

The discrepancy is of little significance save that the passages allowing a long time are probably later in date than those that allot a single night; the interval gave the poet some time for forgetting. Yet the chief import of the difference is to be found in Milton's absorption in his allegories, whether of Sin and Death or of the three days of celestial conflict, which he developed according to probability with little thought of temporal details used elsewhere.

46. Early Rising
(IV. 623-25; V. 2, 139)

AFTER talking on labor as a sign of human dignity, Adam declares:

> To morrow ere fresh Morning streak the East
> With first approach of light, we must be ris'n,
> And at our pleasant labour.   (IV. 623-25)

But like many who resolve on early rising the night before, Adam is not so early as he had planned. When he wak't, at his usual time, morn had already "sow'd the earth with Orient Pearle" (v. 2). It is light enough for him to behold Eve's beauty (v. 14), and to tell her that "the morning shines." When they leave their bower, after some conversation, the sun has just risen (v. 139). On the second morning of which we are told, they rise at the same time (IX. 192).

There seems no special significance in this. In his first speech Adam is emphasizing the need for labor. The later passages give the fact, incidentally allowing Milton to describe the morning as he could not if Adam and Eve came out before light.

47. The Fruits of Experience in Adam and Eve
(IV. 453-69; VIII. 352-54; XI. 277)

IT HAS BEEN at various times observed that Adam and Eve, though they have spent but a short time on earth and have seen nothing of civilization, are generally far from naïve. Milton's poetic purpose required him to make them representatives of the human race, not to try to set forth beings so situated that they cannot learn by imitation but only by their own experience. Indeed the theology of the time declared that Adam was well equipped with knowledge, pointing for an instance of this to his naming of the animals. Adam says:

> I nam'd them, as they pass'd, and understood
> Thir Nature, with such knowledg God endu'd
> My sudden apprehension.   (VIII. 352-54)

Eve, as Adam's other self, has the same intellectual powers, though adapted to her different temperament. If her husband is a zoologist, she is a botanist, for she names the flowers (XI. 277) and we must suppose understood their nature as he did that of the animals. Raphael recognizes Adam's knowledge when he says: "For of armies thou hast heard" (VII. 296).

Yet Milton does at times represent them as inexperienced. Above all they are uncertain about Death. Adam first remarks:

> what ere Death is,
> Som dreadful thing no doubt.   (IV. 425-26)

Later Eve realizes that it means that she would "be no more," would be "extinct" (IX. 827-29), and that they can supply the office of Death with their own hands (X. 1001). When Adam sees the murder of Abel he supposes it the only way to die, and Michael must demonstrate to him other forms of death (XI. 459 ff.).

When first created Adam is in a state of wonderment but not at a loss:

> to speak I tri'd, and forthwith spake,
> My Tongue obey'd and readily could name
> What e're I saw.   (VIII. 271-73)

Eve has more difficulty:

> A murmuring sound
> Of waters issu'd from a Cave and spread
> Into a liquid Plain, then stood unmov'd
> Pure as th' expanse of Heav'n; I thither went
> With unexperienc't thought, and laid me downe
> On the green bank, to look into the cleer
> Smooth Lake, that to me seemd another Skie.
> As I bent down to look, just opposite,
> A Shape within the watry gleam appeerd
> Bending to look on me, I started back,
> It started back, but pleas'd I soon return'd,
> Pleas'd it returnd as soon with answering looks
> Of sympathie and love; there I had fixt
> Mine eyes till now, and pin'd with vain desire,
> Had not a voice thus warnd me, What thou seest,
> What there thou seest fair Creature is thy self,
> With thee it came and goes.   (IV. 453-69)

This is Milton's chief concession to those who demand that Adam and Eve on their first days in the world should be unsophisticated.

48. Eve Retires
(VIII. 48-58)

AFTER THE account of the Creation, Eve, seeing that Adam is entering on further "studious thoughts abstruse," rises and goes among her flowers.[1] It seems then to have occurred to the poet that in this very book Eve is created that Adam might have

> fellowship
> . . . . fit to participate
> All rational delight,   (VIII. 389-91)

such as Milton himself asked for in his writings on divorce. It was, then, hardly the thing to represent her as frightened by the appearance of abstruse thought; indeed Milton did not believe that she would be; hence he wrote:

> Yet went she not, as not with such discourse
> Delighted, or not capable her eare
> Of what was high: such pleasure she reserv'd,
> Adam relating, she sole Auditress;
> Her Husband the Relater she preferr'd
> Before the Angel, and of him to ask
> Chose rather; hee, she knew would intermix
> Grateful digressions, and solve high dispute
> With conjugal Caresses, from his Lip
> Not Words alone pleas'd her. O when meet now
> Such pairs, in Love and mutual Honour joyn'd? (VIII. 48-58)

On the omission of these verses, those preceding and following seem to make excellent sequence. The effect is as though the lines quoted were thrust into the passage to keep it from producing a wrong effect and to enable Milton to assert intellectual quality—suitable to a woman —for Eve.[2]

---

1. For a possible shift in the position of Eve's retirement see Sec. 19, above.

2. For the insertion of a passage into *Comus*, see Fig. 4.

49. The Length of Man's Stay in the Garden
(IV. 449; IX. 63-67; X. 103-8; XI. 317-22; XII. 376-79)

ACCORDING TO Dante, man remained about six hours in the Garden
of Eden. Milton gives him a stay of at least three nights, one when
Satan is found at the ear of Eve, one after Raphael's visit, and one after
the Fall, marked by cold and damp; on the day following the third
they are expelled. These three days, however, seem not to cover man's
time in the Garden. Eve, telling of her experience after creation, speaks
as though at some distance from it, saying: "That day I oft remember"
(IV. 449) and she tells Adam: "I oft am wont" to dream of thee
(V. 32). As though she had had experience with many nights, she says:
"Such night till this I never pass'd" (V. 31). With a similar suggestion
of habit, Milton himself tells that they

> Thir Orisons, each Morning duly paid
> In various style.   (V. 145-46)

Eve and Adam have "oft seen" angels (V. 56; IV. 680-84).[1] Adam says
to Michael on the day after the Judgment, which involved the promise
of the woman's seed:

> Now clear I understand
> What oft my steddiest thoughts have searcht in vain,
> Why our great expectation should be call'd
> The seed of Woman.[2]   (XII. 376-79)

There is no indication that Adam had thought of the matter before he
said that morning to Eve:

> Calling to minde with heed
> Part of our Sentence, that thy Seed shall bruise
> The Serpents head.   (X. 1030-32)

Indeed he knew of it only after the judgment of the preceding evening.
Is his insistence on prolonged thought other than a way of expressing
his great interest? The earlier uses of the word *oft* are perhaps akin to
the habit of the Elizabethan dramatists of using two calendars, so that
events are treated as close together or widely separated as it suits the

---

1. Cf. X. 119; IX. 423.   2. Cf. VIII. 25.

authors. In the passages in *Paradise Lost*, the effect is of something familiar to the speaker; perhaps no further explanation should be sought.

A long time is also implied in the references to God's visits to man. Walking in the Garden before the Judgment after the Fall, God calls aloud:

> Where art thou *Adam*, wont with joy to meet
> My coming seen far off? I miss thee here,
> Not pleas'd, thus entertaind with solitude,
> Where obvious dutie erewhile appear'd unsaught:
> Or come I less conspicuous, or what change
> Absents thee, or what chance detains?   (X. 103-8)

When Adam professes himself afraid, the Judge answers:

> My voice thou oft hast heard, and hast not fear'd,
> But still rejoyc't, how is it now become
> So dreadful to thee?   (X. 119-21)

Adam reinforces this suggestion of many visits by divinity:

> Here I could frequent,
> With worship, place by place where he voutsaf'd
> Presence Divine, and to my Sons relate;
> On this Mount he appeerd, under this Tree
> Stood visible, among these Pines his voice
> I heard, here with him at this Fountain talk'd.[3]   (XI. 317-22)

Yet Milton actually relates but one such visit, that for the Creation, when God held colloquy with Adam and promised him Eve (VIII. 312-455).

How long Adam and Eve remained in Paradise can be in some fashion reckoned. Satan and his followers when driven from Heaven fell nine days (VI. 871). On the burning lake they lay

> Nine times the Space that measures Day and Night
> To mortal men.   (I. 50-51)

Satan then spent some time in his council and in his journey through Hell. His difficult voyage, well nigh to Heaven, of the duration of

---

3. Cf., for later visits, VII. 565-71; XII. 48.

which we are told nothing, presumably was not made more swiftly than his fall, even if we believe Moloc's assertion that the rebel angels went up more easily than down (II. 75-81). That would add nine days more. It is then at least twenty-seven days after Satan's fall before he appears in the Garden. There is no indication that the Almighty did not proceed to Creation as soon as Satan fell. If so, he would have finished before the rebel angels reached Hell. But Raphael on the Sixth Day of Creation, went "on excursion toward the Gates of Hell," and

> Fast we found, fast shut
> The dismal Gates, and barricado'd strong.   (VIII. 240-41)

Evidently the ninth day of fall preceded the sixth of Creation. In the Argument of Book I this is indicated as possible. Satan is "now fallen into Hell, describ'd here, not in the Center (for Heaven and Earth may be suppos'd as yet not made, certainly not yet accurst)." The alternative indicates that Milton was not taking very seriously the relative dates of various actions. In the Argument for Book III, we read that "God sitting on his Throne sees Satan flying towards this world, then newly created." What *newly* means may be debated; if it indicates that God has just returned from Creation,[4] the Creation must have been delayed until Satan was ready to issue from Hell; in that case his upward journey could not have lasted nine days. Milton does not say anywhere that any of the days in question are more than those of "mortal men,"[5] though in Heaven there are such days "as Heav'ns great Year brings forth" (V. 583). Adam and Eve might then have had a couple of weeks in the Garden before the Temptation. Perhaps this is enough to justify *oft*.

There is further indication of time for Satan. After he left the angelic guards on seeing "his mounted scale aloft,"

4. See Sec. 20, above.
5. But cf. *Doctrina Christiana* 1.33 (Columbia ed., XVI, 359): "Dies pro quovis tempore saepe intelligitur." I have throughout taken the word *day* in a simple sense, in deference to Milton's statement: "Certe motum et tempus, quae mensura motus est, secundum prius et posterius, ante mundum hunc conditum esse non potuisse, quod vulgo creditur, nihil cogit assentiri; cum Aristotele in hoc mundo, quem aeternum esse statuit, dari nihilominus motum atque tempus docuerit" (1.7; Columbia ed. XV, 34).

> The space of seven continu'd Nights he rode
> With darkness, thrice the Equinoctial Line
> He circl'd, four times cross'd the Carr of Night
> From Pole to Pole, traversing each Colure;
> On the eighth return'd.   (IX. 63-67)

This indicates the fourth day. Yet the impression given by the rest of
the poem is that Raphael spent with Adam the afternoon of the day
following Satan's capture and that the Temptation came on the next
day; at least no indications of lapse of time are given. If Milton is not
interested in consistency of time, the difference is of no importance; if
exact correspondence is demanded throughout the work, the Temptation must have been postponed until the fourth night, thus lengthening the stay in the Garden by that amount.

It has appeared, however, that to get the result of some three weeks
in the Garden—or probably any other that may be arrived at—one
must estimate some time for periods of whose length Milton tells nothing, as that from Satan's rising from the Lake of Fire to his appearance
on Earth, and that there is difficulty about the days of Creation and
Satan's fall. The truth seems to be that the figures Milton gives are not
intended to be used in this way and that when he does not give the
length of time involved in an action he is not interested in our attempting to reckon it; it is not part of the poem. The numbers given
are virtually round numbers, for the sake of effect; it pleased him to
use nine for Satan, but he did not intend it to be compared with the
Biblically fixed Six Days of Creation. Nor is it necessary to insist on *oft*
as consistently applied to the stay of our first parents in the Garden.
The general impression is that the two in Paradise did not feel anything of novelty about their situation. When the effect of a long stay
is clearly desired, we need only accept it. When Milton tells us nothing about time spent, we do not need to ask; in fact we cannot if we
are to observe the artist's conditions.

CHAPTER EIGHT

THE BUILDING OF *PARADISE LOST*

50. A Table Showing Sequence in Composition

IN THE following table I endeavor to give the sequence of composition of parts of *Paradise Lost*, as it has been presented above. The table is tentative rather than absolute. Some of the parts probably underwent several revisions, widely separated in time. The table has been prepared on the assumption that parts of the epic clearly foreshadowed in the drafts of tragedies may be called essentially early, as having taken form in their author's mind or on his paper, or both, to such an extent that they were not wholly transformed by subsequent revision. Material not mentioned in any of the outlines and apparently inserted in the epic after it was formed has been indicated as late.

No attempt has been made to deal with mere references, such as the line

> Till good Josiah drove them thence to Hell,   (I. 418)

which reminds one of the tragic subject *Josiah Aiaζomenos* (II Kings 23).

Nothing is implied as to the relative time of composing passages within any one of the six groups.[1] The parts of the first group follow the order of Draft Four in the Cambridge Manuscript. The arrangement within the other groups follows the present order of *Paradise Lost*.

---

1. See Sec. 35 for the probability that in Group VI the Council (II. 1-506) is earlier than the anointing of the Son (V. 577-693, 715-802).

THE ORDER OF COMPOSITION OF PARTS OF *Paradise Lost*

GROUP I. *From the Early Tragedies on the Fall (parts based on plans in the Cambridge Manuscript)*

IV. 268-85, 539-49.	The Garden (described by the Chorus in Plan Three and by Gabriel in Plan Four; see Group III, third item, below).
VIII. 457-520.	The creation of Eve and the love and marriage of Adam and Eve (related by Gabriel in Plan Four; in Plans Two and Three, Evening Star (*P.L.*, VIII. 519) is an actor, and in Plan Three the Chorus sing the marriage song).
IV. 8-31, 42-130, 356-94, 505-38; IX. 99-178.	Satan bemoaning himself and contriving Adam's ruin (Plans Three and Four).
IV. 869-1015.	Satan and the angelic guards (Plan Four; see also Group IV, below).
X. 474-501.	Satan "relating and insulting in what he had don to the destruction of man" (Plan Four).
IX. 1067-1189.	Adam and Eve feel guilt after the Fall (Plan Four).
X. 720-908.	Adam and Eve quarrel (Plan Four).
III. 93-134, 203-10.	God's justice proved (Plan Four).
XI. 193-369.	The coming of Michael (Plans Three and Four).
XI. 466-552.	Sickness (Plans One, Two, Three, and Four).
XII. 270-484	Promise of the Messiah (Plan Four, the tragedies on King David and *Christus patiens*[2] in the Cambridge Manuscript).
XII. 485-649.	Adam is instructed and comforted, repents, gives God the glory, submits (Plans Three and Four).

2. See Fig. 3.

GROUP II. *From Other Early Tragedies (parts based on plans in the Cambridge Manuscript)*

X. 649-719.	Change in climate (*Adam in Banishment*).
XI. 134-192.	Adam and Eve after the Fall (*Adam in Banishment*).
XI. 423-65.	Cain and Abel (*Adam in Banishment*).
XI. 637-901.	The Flood (*The Flood* or *The Deluge*).
XII. 111-54.	Abraham (tragedies on Abram).
XII. 260-69.	Joshua (tragedies on Joshua).

GROUP III. *From the Late Tragedy (parts perhaps based on Plan Five, that mentioned by Edward Phillips)*

IV. 1-8.	Adam and Eve need warning.
IV. 32-41.	Satan's address to the Sun (specified by Phillips).
IV. 132-71, 205-68.	The Garden (probably retaining something from Plan Four; see Group I, first item, above).
IV. 288-355, 408-504, 598-775.	Adam and Eve in the Garden.
IV. 549-97.	Uriel warns the guards.
V. 1-8, 11-25, 136-219.	Adam and Eve in the Garden.
X. 909-1104.	Adam and Eve reconciled and penitent.

GROUP IV. *Tragedy Transformed to Epic (parts primarily epic but with some dependence on the tragedies of the Cambridge Manuscript)*

IV. 776-99, 823-68.	Satan and the angelic guards (see also Group I, above).
V. 694-714.	War in Heaven (a choric song in Plans Three and Four).[3] (See also Group VI, the anointing of the Son as the cause of Satan's rebellion.)

VI. 44-98, 202-669.	War in Heaven (a choric song in Plans Three and Four).[3]
VII. 131-640.	The Creation (a choric song in Plans Three and Four).[3]
VIII. 204-456, 521-643.	The Creation (a choric song in Plans Three and Four).[3]
IX. 48-98; 179-1066.	The Fall (related by an angel in Plan Four).[3]

GROUP V. *The Independent Epic (parts not suggested in the plans for tragedies and probably not planned until the epic form was settled on)*

I. 1-669.	Satan in Hell.
II. 629-648, 884-1055.	Satan's voyage.
III. 56-92.	Satan observed from Heaven.
III. 418-742.	Satan's voyage.
IV. 172-204.	Satan as cormorant.
IV. 395-408.	Satan as a beast of prey.
IV. 799-822.	Satan like a toad.
V. 219-560.	Raphael's visit.
V. 561-76.	Raphael's prelude.
VI. 894-912.	Adam warned against Satan by Raphael.
VII. 40-130.	Adam's desire for knowledge.
VIII. 644-53.	Raphael departs.
X. 1-228.	The Son as judge.
X. 332-44.	Adam and Eve and the Serpent judged.
XI. 1-133.	God sends Michael to expel Adam and Eve from the Garden.
XI. 370-422.	Geographical prospect.

3. In spite of the greater length and varied form of the passage in the epic, some lines may have remained from the tragedy.

XI. 552-636.	The Arts and the Sons of God.
XII. 1-110.	Nimrod.
XII. 155-260.	Israel in Egypt and the Exodus.

GROUP VI. *The Epic Complete (parts substituted for earlier passages or inserted when the poem seemed finished)*

I. 670-798.	Pandaemonium.
II. 1-520.	The council (a substitute for that mentioned in the Argument of Book I).
II. 521-628.	Hell as a universe.
II. 648-884.	Sin and Death (Sin is not mentioned in the tragic drafts; Death possibly owes something to the early plans, as in being armed, according to one convention, with a dart— *P.L.* II. 672, 702, 729, 786; XI. 491).
III. 1-55.	Blindness.
III. 135-202, 210-417.	Free will, predestination, redemption.
V. 8-11, 26-135.	Eve's dream.
V. 577-693, 715-802.	The anointing of the Son as the cause of Satan's rebellion.
V. 803-907.	Abdiel.
VI. 1-43, 99-202.	Abdiel.
VI. 669-893.	Messiah's victory (substituted for an earlier victory by the angels).
VII. 1-39.	Milton "with dangers compast round."
VIII. 1-204.	Astronomy.
IX. 1-47.	Milton on the heroic poem.
X. 229-331, 345-414, 585-648.	Sin and Death.
X. 414-473, 502-84.	Satan and Hell.

51. Milton's Process

OF THE GROUPS of the preceding section, the first, following the plans
in the Cambridge Manuscript, when united with Group III gives much
of the material that presumably was to be found in the tragedy of
which Edward Phillips read the opening lines. The lines number about
2,150. The matter in the choric songs (Group IV) would obviously
have added three or four hundred verses, bringing the total to about
2,500, less than one-half longer than *Samson Agonistes,* with its 1,758
lines. If Milton had allowed himself Shakespearean scope he could
have gone above 3,000 lines. Unless he wholly abandoned his view
that the three Greek dramatists offer the best models for tragedy, he
can hardly have gone so far, certainly not to the 4,278 lines of
Andreini's *Adamo.*[1] However much the passages possibly derived
from a play have been revised, their total is such as at least not to
destroy belief in an underlying tragedy of about 2,500 lines.

The relation between Group I and the epic is apparent. The outline of action is in the same sequence. The portions out of the epic
order, such as the section of Book VIII coming early in the group, are
not part of the basic action, but have an episodic position in the
tragedy as later in the heroic poem. They were easily shifted to fit the
different plan of the longer work.

The more extensive epic plan required that some portions present
in the tragedy be handled in greater detail. Milton might have presented at the end of *Paradise Lost* a long array of figures "in manner
of a mask, enranged orderly," as Spenser did; in fact he does almost
retain the masque, though greatly expanding the stage, for the actors
of early Biblical history "passe before his eyes," as the fourth draft
puts it, in "the visions of God" (XI. 377). When the allegorical figures
of War and Sickness and the others were replaced by the Biblical
scenes, any verses already composed for tragedies taken from Genesis
(Group II) were ready at hand.

If the tragedy after the fifth plan differed from its predecessor in
being somewhat longer and in proceeding by action more than by
narration, its outline was doubtless most modified at the beginning,
with Satan's immediate appearance instead of the preparation for him

1. To be sure many lines of this work are short, as "A dar vita" (2981).

made in Plan Four. The additional matter assigned to this last tragedy (Group III) is confined to the fourth and fifth books of *Paradise Lost;* the description of the Garden presumably was woven into the action in the manner of Shakespeare rather than given to a formal speaker, such as a prologizer or chorus.

On laying hold of the material in Group IV Milton first had the epic problem to grapple with. The tragic outline was to be abandoned and the material transformed from the brief chorus to the long narrative. Composition must be virtually independent of what had earlier been planned and written.

The details of Milton's procedure up to this point are quite unknown. Without doubt he prepared for his heroic poem an outline quite as elaborate as those for the tragedies. If any inference may be drawn from the Arguments,[2] it was even longer, since their total length is seven times that of the outline of *Adam unparadiz'd.* There is little indication that Milton consulted Draft Four when preparing the argument of *Paradise Lost*, though there are a few verbal similarities.[3] However dependent he was on the tragedy, he would have thought out the new work as an epic, with ruthless abandonment of anything that did not fit his new plan. His success is made evident by the immediate and continuing acceptance of his work as an epic.[4]

The detailed composition of passages in any way derived from the tragedy we know almost nothing about. Did Milton have his secretary read to him from his manuscripts or did he use the earlier works only as he remembered them? Exact copying is suggested by the passage quoted by Edward Phillips as the beginning of the tragedy, since it differs (except for spelling and punctuation) from the text of the fourth book of *Paradise Lost* in but one word; probably, however, Phillips made a mistake in copying from the printed text. Would he have quoted so exactly from memory? His account makes clear that he was not present at the actual dictation of any verses; he saw only the finished form in parcels of "Ten, Twenty, or Thirty Verses at a Time," and corrected the "Orthography and Pointing."[5] His words

2. See Sec. 3, above.
3. *Ibid.*
4. May I again remind the reader that my analysis of Milton's methods does not mean that I

regard the final *Paradise Lost* as other than gorgeously successful?
5. Helen Darbishire, *Early Lives of Milton*, p. 73.

do not suggest the taking over of finished verses from an old manuscript. Indeed it is not to be supposed that any portions so used were
not revised and adapted to their new surroundings. If in addition they
were taken not from paper but from the poet's memory, the modification may have been considerable. Phillips, however, was not con-
tinuously with his uncle but only went to visit him "from time to
time," so that his knowledge may have covered only part of the work.

When the passages in Group IV had been written down, the
material thought out for the tragedy was, except for incidental bits,
exhausted, even to the choric songs. The transformation to the heroic
poem was achieved and the plot stood independent, though the central
action of the Fall, demanded by the tragedy, made the heroic poem
dramatic rather than epic at heart. The epic gave more chance than
the tragedy for insistence on the world-wide and time-striding importance of Adam's action. For such an effect Milton shifted from a
masque of evils to the prospect over the whole world in Book XI, not
confined to one royal or ducal family but covering all the globe

>   wherever stood
>   City of old or modern Fame,   (xi. 385-86)

and instinct with the brotherhood of man. This and other passages in
Group V were now written. Some of them were pure additions permitted by a shift in order, as Adam's expression of his desire for
knowledge, made fitting when the Book of the Creation became
number seven. Others made some transformation possible; without
the narrative by Raphael, the War in Heaven could hardly have become an episode. Completely new is the bulk of the first book, probably not developed to its present form, and Satan's voyage in Books
II and III. Nothing of the sort was contemplated in the tragedy; Plan
Four says that "Lucifer appears after his overthrow"; there is no possibility for a narrative of exploits in Hell, unless very briefly when
Lucifer "bemoans himself." With the fifth group, the poem may be
considered to have assumed much of its characteristic quality.

The components of Group V are striking in view of the 19th
century criticism which—tacitly or openly—held the first two books
the most "Miltonic" part of *Paradise Lost*. Any one who still holds
that view may find in my analysis a new reason for it, namely that after

the experience of writing the greater part of *Paradise Lost* Milton was at the summit of his poetical powers. Similarly one who wishes to depreciate the eleventh and twelfth books can support his views by suggesting early planning and composition.

The sixth group saw the poet still writing important passages, though usually by way of substitution or insertion rather than addition of new matter on a large scale. He was looking for inadequate sections and attempting to strengthen them. Presumably the earlier council of Satan and his lieutenants was somewhat Tassian; wishing to make plainer the apparent democracy and real tyranny of Satan, Milton discarded it for what we now have. Abdiel too served to emphasize the irrational quality of Satan's rebellion as nothing had earlier done; when writing the Seraph's speeches Milton probably supposed he was anticipating that sympathy with Satan's position as a rebel which, as the event has shown, even such passages have failed to make impossible.[6] Messiah's victory enabled Milton to go somewhat further than otherwise toward his ideal epic, in which wars are not the main thing; he could also assert in a new way his theme of the divine power. The introductions to Books III, VII, and IX enabled him to speak of himself—thus gaining further variety.

While all this was going on, there was also much revision of verbal details such as the Cambridge Manuscript shows he applied to some of his earlier writings,[7] though few traces of such detailed revision now survive. The trifling alterations in the manuscript of the first book used by the printer,[8] and the slight additions for the second edition are in striking contrast to the hundreds of changes made by Ariosto for his second edition and the hundreds more for his third. Is it possible that Milton did not have the whole reread to him that he might make final revisions? Could it have been given to the printer with no further correction, after Edward Phillips had made changes in spelling in the groups of ten, twenty, and thirty lines of which he

6. This appears in the objections to Mr. C. S. Lewis' *Preface to Paradise Lost* raised by Mr. C. Rostrevor Hamilton in *Hero or Fool? A Study of Milton's Satan*, and Mr. Elmer Edgar Stoll in "Give the Devil his Due," *The Review of English Studies*, XX (1944), 108-24.

7. See Figs. 4 and 5.

8. See *The Manuscript of Milton's Paradise Lost, Book I*, ed. Helen Darbishire (Oxford, 1931); Harris F. Fletcher, *Milton's Works in Photographic Facsimile* (Urbana, 1945), II, 31-99.

speaks? It should be kept in mind that Phillips tells the story for the purpose of showing at what time of year Milton composed, rather than to give general information about his methods of writing. Milton evidently was obliged to adapt his process to his blindness.

Any material that the poet thriftily retained from his earlier efforts must have undergone many changes before it satisfied him in detail and fitted into its new place. Even one able, as Milton apparently was,[9] to print youthful work with little change must sometimes have made modifications so great as to displace much of the original. To say that Milton is using early material may mean at the utmost that he had his secretary transcribe from an early manuscript; at the least it may mean only that a plan made long before was finally executed. There is little possibility of telling which process lies behind any single passage.

The process of growth that has been described—growth from the first draft for *Paradise Lost,* or even from the ambitions mentioned in *At a Vacation Exercise*—is to be considered in relation to what may be thought the disjointed effect produced by the attempt to date the various parts of the epic. To some extent the poem is the result of shifting matter and inserting it. Some disadvantageous effects of that process remain, though the total result of every shift and insertion was greater excellence. Yet the metamorphosis was under the control of a central purpose, clear at the outset, growing clearer as time went on, but gaining complete clarity only when the *Paradise Lost* we know was complete. The fourth draft represents a full-wrought unit. Yet it was inadequate to satisfy its author's growing vision of his end. Though abandoned for the epic plan, it still furnished the center around which later work was grouped. It yielded, moreover, to a long-considered epic scheme. Transformation or shifting of its parts—large or small—was always controlled by design. Additional parts demanded by the epic form were also subordinated to the ruling intention, and after they were thought out might be restricted, shifted, or rejected for more adequate successors. The last additions also, as they fulfilled intentions latent from the beginning but emergent only as the process drew to its close, took the places demanded by the

9. The printed forms of early work he allowed to remain unaltered. There is less certainty about early work that remained long in manuscript, such as the additions in the volume of 1673.

nature of the work. The patchy effect of the details when viewed one by one disappears when they are seen as components of the grand design.

No classification of Milton's changes and additions can be absolute. They were all intended to develop the design in its entirety as it grew clearer with the years, and all are involved with all the various aspects of the poem. So far as they can be separated, they may be called alterations for idea, for construction, and for elaboration. A few representative modifications may be classified.

Largely for the sake of the theological idea, Milton brought Messiah into the War in Heaven. The battle in its earlier form was a struggle among the angels not unlike a Homeric battle, and with no more meaning than the contests of the *Iliad*. Milton found himself approaching what in theory he rejected:

> to dissect
> With long and tedious havoc fabl'd Knights
> In Battels feign'd. (IX. 29–31)

When the Son is victor, the emphasis is put on the divine power and its absolute supremacy over Satan. Belief in omnipotence was cardinal to Milton's personal creed and one of the chief matters his poem justifies. Likewise added to the War in Heaven is Abdiel, who gives opportunity for further expression of the Almighty's government, this time in the dynamic theological speeches of the fearless angel. Milton's beliefs were probably the same when he wrote of a mere angelic war as when he had brought the fifth and sixth books to their present state, but his changes added greatly to the intellectual content of those books and cut down the emphasis on war, which he thought not the most heroic of subjects.

A different type of insertion, for the sake of a subordinate idea, is that on Eve's retirement, where it is asserted that Eve was delighted with abstruse discussion and that her ear was capable of what was high.[10] This fits with much in *Paradise Lost*, where Milton, so far from showing the "Turkish contempt" for women that long has been assigned to him, takes some pains to represent Eve in an admirable light, as though to atone for the prominent part she takes in the Fall. The

10. See Sec. 48, above.

poet not only makes her initiative in the "self-condemning" bring peace between her and Adam, but reminds his reader of her share in the final overthrow of Satan.[11] Though retaining the Pauline view of the subordination of women, Milton gives her intellectual capacity worthy of Adam's respect. Not only is she Adam's "other self" as a friend "fit to participate All rational delight,"[12] but she has such knowledge that she can name the flowers (XI. 277) as Adam named the animals and "understood Thir Nature" (VIII. 352-53). Since this giving of suitable names by Adam was understood by theologians as symbolizing general intellectual power, the same is to be assumed for Eve when she gives names. Holding such an opinion of Eve's powers not merely as botanist but as thinker in all respects, Milton took the opportunity to assert this in a context that might otherwise receive the opposite interpretation. He was, however, still careful to make Eve's intellectual enjoyment dependent on Adam and associated with specifically feminine qualities. Thus he gave expression to an idea that he had held for years and that had from the first been latent in the epic.

The great change for the sake of construction is the moving of the War in Heaven from the beginning of the poem and making it part of the angel's narrative. The gain in compactness was great. Milton could now feel that he had found an Aristotelian beginning for his action, and was truly plunging *in medias res*. The change of the book of the Creation, now the seventh, also shortened the material essentially prefatory and brought Satan earlier into the Garden on his mission, so that the essential action could begin with the fourth book. This transfer of the Creation was the more needed when Book III was expanded with material of import, though not part of the main action, such as the speeches on the Plan of Salvation. Artistic reasons may be given for the insertion of the scenes in Hell and Chaos in Book X; they balance the similar scenes at the beginning of the poem and break up the section giving the drama of Adam and Eve, which otherwise would occupy almost all of Books IX and X.

To desire for elaboration and variety may be attributed the insertion of Sin and Death in the second book. They are unnecessary to the

11. *P.L.*, X. 909-36, 1031; XI. 116, 155; XII. 601. See Allan H. Gilbert, "Milton on the Position of Woman," Part II, *Modern Language Review*, XV (1920), 240-64.

12. VIII. 390-91, 450, 495.

action; indeed it has even been remarked that they are curiously unsuitable for keeping safe the gates of Hell; yet the description of them is one of the oft-quoted parts of the poem. Likewise the great series of speeches that begins Book II has no real effect on the fate of man; that, as to the devils, depends on Satan alone. Yet the poem would be much less rich without this display of diabolical rhetoric. Milton rightly felt that the closely knit central portion of his epic, derived from a highly-unified tragedy, permitted him to use within his framework what episodes he would to enhance his total effect.

52. Labor and Intent Study

THREE FAMOUS poems, related to *Paradise Lost,* have been studied in a fashion akin to that used above: the *Aeneid, Orlando Furioso,* and the *Faerie Queene.*[1]

The *Aeneid,* though an apparent unit, did not satisfy its author, who is reported to have given directions that it be burned, or at least that only parts he had himself approved should be given to the world.[2] If it is also true that he intended to give three years to further revision, he would have approved the circulation of but little of it—not even of the books he is reported to have read to Augustus.

The arrangement of the first six books in an early stage was III, V, I, II, IV, VI. Later the first four had the order III, I, II, IV. Some of the changes in plan involved much rewriting; for example, the present Book V is much changed from its original state as Book II. The present Book III, believed older than most of the others, since it is in various ways inconsistent with them, would have been much revised if the poet's life had not been cut short. His early editors, Varius and Tucca, may have "found the book actually marked for rejection. . . . It is possible that they did find it so marked, but decided to include it rather than leave a gap in the story. Its inclusion would involve no real disloyalty to Vergil's memory, for its suppression would have greatly weakened the *Aeneid* as a whole."[3]

1. Something of the same method has appeared in the study of other works, such as the *Iliad,* Sidney's *Arcadia,* and even the Book of Job.
2. Marjorie Crump, *The Growth of* the *Aeneid* (Oxford, 1920). Miss Crump, like the authors of the studies of the other two poets, is much indebted to earlier workers.
3. *Ibid.,* p. 39.

Ariosto has left the clearest evidence of his long labors.[4] The printed text that he brought out in 1521 is superficially little different from that of 1516; for the most part the two editions correspond, stanza for stanza. Yet some three quarters of the stanzas underwent revision, ranging from a different spelling of a single word to a complete rewriting, though without change in general sentiment. Nor was this the end. The process of improving the stanza without modifying its relation to the whole was carried even further in the edition of 1532. Most of the octaves left untouched in 1521 were then altered, so that few stand in the last edition as in the first. Moreover, many of those once revised were further altered. But this scrutiny of every line in the poem was not all. Some seven hundred verses were inserted into the narrative, increasing the total number of cantos by six. Two important characters and many lesser ones were introduced for the first time, though none of them was carried beyond the limits of the inserted matter.

Manuscripts of most, though not all, of the material added in 1532 have survived, some of them in two forms, one heavily revised, the other a less revised transcript of the first. Some of the pages show shifting of the order of stanzas. Moreover, these manuscripts tell but part of the story. Even the copies now most marked up seem to have been set down as though in final form, with the belief that they would receive but slight revision thereafter; how many copies went before we can only infer.

Though these printed and manuscript pages represent Ariosto's vast labor in revision, they also have value in hinting what went on before 1516 when the poet was selecting his material, composing his verses in their first form, and arranging the forty cantos of the plot. Not improbably many pages of manuscript were thrown aside as unsatisfactory.[5] The labor of arranging the acceptable material was complex. Some events probably at first intended for early parts of the work now appear near the middle. Planning and change were continuous until the poem was in print. For example, the love of Angelica and Medoro, now one of the striking parts of the poem, seems to be

4. Allan H. Gilbert, "Weaving the Web of *Orlando Furioso*," a paper read before the Romance Section of the Modern Language Association on December 28, 1944 (unpublished).

5. The *Cinque Canti*, much disputed, seem to me of early composition.

the result of a late change. Originally Medoro was slain. Then Ariosto decided to let Angelica heal his wounds and fall in love with him. In adapting this new action to the poem as it stood, he hurriedly wrote necessary linking verses. One stanza resulting from this is probably the most vapid in the poem.[6] Other changes have left similar traces.

Dissatisfied with his last edition, both because of his own failings and those of his printer, Ariosto left a copy, we are told, with revisions for a further edition. He is even believed to have intended to add more cantos. It perhaps is not too much to say that the last edition represents what he had achieved up to its publication, but is not a final form.

The evolution of *The Faerie Queene* was much of the same sort,[7] though Spenser does not show the desire for perfection so obviously as does his Italian master. For example, he undertook no revision of the first three books of his poem for their second printing. Yet his labors had not been short. There was in 1580 a manuscript of *The Faerie Queene*, sufficiently finished to be submitted to his friend Harvey for judgment, though not until 1590 did the first three books appear. Of that early form we know little; it may be an overstatement to say that it was "quite unlike any part of the poem in the shape it ultimately took."[8] Parts probably have survived from it, however much the whole has been changed. It is easy to suppose that this early poem gave more opportunity than the present one for Gabriel Harvey to write to the author: "You wil needes seeme to emulate, and hope to overgo [*Orlando Furioso*], as you flatly professed your self in one of your last Letters." It is likely that Gabriel saw a poem not divided into books as at present, but in continuous cantos. The stories of the various knights were not given the prominence they receive from books devoted to them but were woven into the narrative wherever they seemed effective. Above all, though there may have been more allegory than in Ariosto's work, there was much less than in the present *Faerie Queene*. If so, Spenser's great change was the adoption of the arrangement in books each devoted—at least ostensibly—to a

6. *Orlando Furioso*, 12.65. The function of the stanza is to say that Angelica found the wounded Medoro. This occupies but three lines; the rest is of little value.

7. Bennett, *The Evolution of "The Faerie Queene."*

8. George L. Craik, *Spenser, and His Poetry* (London, 1845), I, 105.

virtue. This required the strengthening of allegorical passages already
written, the insertion of new ones, and rearrangement of the considerable parts of the earlier poem he retained. It is no wonder that
the leisure of the next ten years was required for the completion of
three books, and six years more for the next three.

Even then the neat plan of twelve cantos of about the same length
devoted to a knight personifying a virtue is not uniformly carried
out. The writer best informed on this matter holds that the Herculean
task Spenser undertook was too great for the time at his command.
Achieving high quality in individual verse and in various parts of his
structure—even of Books I and II entire—he did not have time
enough for mastering the whole. "It is not incompetence but HASTE
that is writ large over the face of the poem's narrative technique."[9]
This judgment, if applied with rigor, I incline to modify. The conflict between the two systems—that of the entire poem as a unit and
that of the poem as made up of twelve distinct books—seems funda-
mental. Ariosto could handle the first; Gower in the *Confessio
Amantis* shows what can be done with the second. The two do not
fuse easily. Could Spenser hope to bring about a real union? But even
if he could not, it is probable that he so improved his poem by using
a new method giving scope to his genius that any faults in structure
are but a small price to pay for what was gained. On the other hand,
it may be that his intention has not been quite correctly analysed, and
that his achievement in Books III and IV was more satisfactory to the
poet himself than is sometimes thought. We do not know that he expressed discontent with any part of his work after it was printed.

In the course of this revising, many inconsistencies came in.[10] For
example, Britomart says:

From the howre
I taken was from nourses tender pap,
I have been trained up in warlike stowre,
To tossen speare and shield, and to affrap
The warlike ryder to his most mishap

. . . .

All my delight on deedes of armes is set
To hunt out perils and adventures hard.   (III. ii. 6, 7)

9. Bennett, *op. cit.,* p. 253.
10. See Bennett, *op. cit.,* Index under *Inconsistencies.*

Yet in the next canto her nurse says to her:

> Let us in feigned armes our selves disguize,
> And our weake hands (whom need new strength shall teach)
> The dreadful speare and shield to exercize:
>
> . . . .· . . . .
>
> Ne ought ye want, but skill, which practize small
> Will bring, and shortly make you a mayd Martiall.   (III. iii. 53)

The first passage suggests a story like that of Bradamante in *Orlando Furioso* xxv. 32, since it expands a speech by that virgin who was both good duke and excellent warrior.[11] The other hints that Britomart is to assume arms only for a special purpose, as did Tasso's Erminia when

> Col durissimo acciar preme ed offende
> Il delicato collo e l'aurea chioma;
> E la tenera man lo scudo prende,
> Pur troppo grave e insopportabil soma,   (VI. 92)

that in such disguise she may seek her lover. Early training "in warlike stowre" fits the career of Britomart as Spenser usually presents her—the equal of Ariosto's heroine. Yet it seems that there was a time when he preferred to liken her to Erminia.

With years and leisure the author might have completed the twelve books he mentioned in the letter to Raleigh. If to the end he considered some such plan essential to his work, he fell much farther short of completion than did Vergil or Ariosto.

Milton perhaps satisfied himself better than any of the others. His life was longer than theirs; when *Paradise Lost* was published he had reached the age at which Ariosto died, fifty-nine. Spenser died at forty-seven, Vergil at fifty-one. Even blindness and the failure of his political party were not wholly damaging, since they acted to secure Milton the leisure Spenser never had. Moreover his task, so far as it can be measured by length, was not much greater than Vergil's, and far less than that of the two romancers. The first edition of his poem was evidently satisfactory to him, since for the second he undertook no general revision, adding only a dozen lines, some of which result from the division of two of the books otherwise unchanged. Yet the poem

---

11. Spenser also draws on Tasso, *Gerusalemme Liberata*, 2.39.

contains such marks of insufficient labor as have been pointed out in earlier sections.

In spite of all this, for these four poems one fact remains. They were triumphant. Thousands of readers of Vergil for centuries had no idea what lines, even what books he especially wished to improve. Ariosto was the popular poet of his age and still stands as one of the greatest Italians. Spenser became the poet's poet of England, the second glory of the greatest age of English verse. English literature without Milton can hardly be imagined. The inconsistencies in all these famous works have been little noticed. So far as I know, very few of Milton's inconsistencies have been previously commented on; he has rather been praised, in the words of Matthew Arnold, for "flawless perfection." The defects revealed by analysis of the four works have been unseen by countless readers and students for generations. So far as pleasure is concerned, they have not existed, do not exist, and, one may add, should not exist. In weighing these poems they have not been even dust in the balance.

After Charles Lamb had seen the crossed-out and rewritten manuscripts of Milton's early work in the library of Trinity College, Cambridge, he wrote:

I had thought of the Lycidas as of a full-grown beauty—as springing up with all its parts absolute—till, in an evil hour, I was shown the original copy of it, together with the other minor poems of its author, in the library of Trinity, kept like some treasure, to be proud of. I wish they had thrown them in the Cam, or sent them after the latter Cantos of Spenser, into the Irish Channel. How it staggered me to see the fine things in their ore! interlined, corrected! as if their words were mortal, alterable, displaceable at pleasure! as if they might have been otherwise, and just as good! as if inspiration were made up of parts, and these fluctuating, successive, indifferent! I will never go into the workshop of any great artist again.[12]

Such an attitude may be satisfactory for a reader; it cannot be held by one who will know the nature of poetry. The history of our four

12. "Essays of Elia," ed. Alfred Ainger (in *Life and Works*, Troy, N. Y., 1899), II. 300. This note appeared only in the *Lon-* *don Magazine;* Lamb struck it out when he collected and printed his essays.

poems is the reverse of rising perfect from a single inspiration. Ariosto supposed at the beginning that he was merely to write additions to *Orlando Innamorato,* Spenser that he could transport Ariosto to his own England, Milton that *Paradise Lost* was to be a tragedy. Such uncertainty, which some may be tempted to call vacillation, such slow and stumbling progress, such dependence on trial and error—can that be the method of the great artist? Did Dante acknowledge it as his own when he wrote of

> il poema sacro,
> Al quale ha posto mano e cielo e terra,
> Sì che m'ha fatto per più anni macro?   *(Par.* 25.1-3)

The method of slow advance, not by clear foresight but by seeing a thing standing complete and then changing it, is not commonly assigned to genius. But is the artist distinguished from ordinary men not so much by mysterious gifts as by his power of discontent and his patience in labor at things both large and small? Would Spenser, if he had published in 1580, have attained little more than did William Warner? Would Ariosto, if his manuscripts had not been so revised and marked for shifting that no one but himself could interpret them, have joined in obscurity the author of *Girone il cortese?* On the other hand, why did Trissino's twenty years of labor produce only *Italia liberata da Gotti?* Evidently the poet must be able not merely to sustain years of labor but also to make continuous application of good judgment. Tasso's critical power seems to have failed when he revised his *Gerusalemme;* the new form, though circulating far more widely than is sometimes supposed, is inferior to that first printed. The poet is great as he has the spirit to master his process and judge his result, even though, as is reported of Milton, he found that between the vernal and the autumnal equinox "whatever he attempted was never to his satisfaction, though he courted his fancy never so much."[13]

If we may infer from our four poems, this power to write and rewrite, to build and unbuild to build once more, is indispensable to the creator of a long poem. Let other gifts be what they will, ten thousand lines that will live—or enough of them to carry the weaker ones—are not produced by a poet who does not have great powers of

13. Edward Phillips, in Darbishire, *Early Lives of Milton,* p. 73.

endurance. His changes are not the result of fickleness, but rather of a steadiness that can mould his product ever nearer to perfection. Temperament may lead him to consider his work finished too soon, as Spenser perhaps did after many years, as though realizing that art was too long for the few and busy seasons to be left to him. Yet the peculiar endowment of any of these poets acts always in relation to their common power for paying in years and toil the price of perfection.

It seems likely that their works contain more inconsistencies than do those of lesser men. If a poet adopts a plan early, if he does not vary from it, he diminishes the likelihood of minor errors. Since the span of time is not long, there is little opportunity for forgetfulness. But to hold every detail for ten years is not easy. If during the ten years a part of the plot has been of one sort, then has been altered, to be altered once more, it is not strange if the memory does not react immediately toward revision of a part of the poem, perhaps of a dozen years standing, that is not in harmony with recent changes. Moreover the great poet is concerned primarily with great matters; however valiantly he bends to details, he will let some of them slip. If the method of these four poets was right, if perfection is attained gradually and by dint of much cutting and trying, the slight flaws of a great work are an index of its quality. If every improvement leaves behind it some trace, the more traces of change we find in an epic, the more it has been bettered. A great man makes many changes, but a lesser artist, who does not repeatedly raise the quality of his works, has no occasion to leave rough bits where once was attached a part now swept away or moved to a better place.

These four poets followed Horace:

> nonumque prematur in annum,
> membranis intus positus: delere licebit
> quod non edideris.   (*Ars Poetica*, 388-90)

To Horatians the poet is the craftsman. As other man work at their trades or professions, the poet labors at his. A cabinetmaker of intelligence and industry will make good furniture, and so with the poet and his verses. Perhaps Foscolo felt something of that when on seeing the scratched and corrected manuscripts of *Orlando Furioso* he did not, like Lamb, regret the sight, but wrote *vide e venerò;* "I saw and worshipped." Yet even Horace mentions inspiration, and Milton, for all his "labor and intent study," makes the poet dependent on "devout prayer to that eternall Spirit who can enrich with all utterance and Knowledge, and sends out his Seraphim with the hallow'd fire of his Altar to touch and purify the lips of whom he pleases."[14]

A theory of perfection removes the artist from the realm of faulty men and makes his poem a work of magic rather than of the human spirit at its best, with intellect and emotion doing all they can. If the poet is a man among men, he has not only bestowed labor on many passages but, however much he has attained, has left other passages on which he might have put additional labor. Icy perfection would mark a poet as inhuman.

14. *The Reason of Church-government,* Bk. 2, Introduction (Columbia ed., III. 241).

INDEX

(Topics, Names, and Passages in *Paradise Lost*)

A